Winning
with
Software

Winning
with
Software

An Executive Strategy

Watts S. Humphrey

✦Addison-Wesley

Boston • San Francisco • New York • Toronto • Montreal
London • Munich • Paris • Madrid
Capetown • Sydney • Tokyo • Singapore • Mexico City

Carnegie Mellon
Software Engineering Institute

The SEI Series in Software Engineering

The publisher offers discounts on this book when ordered in quantity for special sales. For more information, please contact:

U.S. Corporate and Government Sales
(800) 382-3419
corpsales@pearsontechgroup.com

For sales outside of the U.S., please contact:

International Sales
(317) 581-3793
international@pearsontechgroup.com

Visit Addison-Wesley on the Web: www.awprofessional.com

Library of Congress Cataloging-in-Publication Data

Humphrey, Watts S., 1927–
    Winning with software : an executive strategy / Watts S. Humphrey.
        p.   cm.
    Includes bibliographical references and index.
    ISBN 0-201-77639-1
    1. Computers.   2. Electronic data processing.   3. Business—Data processing.   I. Title.

QA76.H7943 2002
005.3—dc21
                                                                    2001053787

ISBN 0-201-77639-1

Text printed in the United States at RR Donnelley Crawfordsville in Crawfordsville, Indiana.

6th Printing July 2007

For my family.
My work has been rewarding,
but nothing beats coming home.

Contents

Preface

When I mention software to senior executives, I get lots of reactions. Most are frustrated. They complain about missed commitments, quality problems, and unpleasant surprises. Others have been less closely involved. Software was a problem, but those problems have been handled. No one mentions the business opportunities of software. They think of software as a necessary evil—something to be avoided if possible. While most executives would agree that the software part of their business is growing very quickly, they never think of it as an asset or an opportunity.

By using the methods described in this book, organizations have transformed their software groups. The first Boeing team cut test time by 94%; an air force group doubled productivity; a Teradyne project delivered a large defect-free product. These and other organizations are getting outstanding results. However, they all started with a management focus on the opportunities with software.

THREAT OR OPPORTUNITY

Software is a truly incredible technology. It has a zero production cost, can be distributed worldwide in seconds, does not wear out or deteriorate, and is the most economical and flexible way to implement almost any complex function. In just about any field of engineering or science, more than half a typical professional's time is now spent in using, developing, enhancing, or maintaining software. By any measure, software is big business.

To visualize the opportunities with software, consider the inverse: potential threats. Take manufacturing, for example. Suppose your leading competitor mastered a technology that cut manufacturing costs in half, eliminated distribution delays, and provided products that never wore out or deteriorated. If you did not quickly capitalize on that technology, you would almost certainly be in trouble. Conversely, think of the opportunities if your organization mastered this technology and your competitors did not. While software is precisely such a technology, few organizations see it as either an opportunity or a threat. The principal reason is that many executives don't think their organizations do much software work and, of those that do, few have enough software knowledge or experience to appreciate how it contributes to their business. Once they think the software problems are under control, they do their best to avoid the subject.

A growing number of executives have found that software is a powerful business asset. However, these same executives have also found that moving into the modern world of engineered software requires an organizational transformation. What is more, they have discovered that they must personally lead this transformation. It is not a simple change and, like all changes, this transformation involves more than just telling people what to do. The best way to explain what is involved is to tell the story of how the methods described in this book were created.

THE TRANSFORMATION JOURNEY

During my 27 years with IBM, one of my jobs was director of programming. I supervised 4,000 software professionals in 15 laboratories and 7 countries. In four years, we took this organization from the brink of chaos to a sound, businesslike operation. The first step was to establish effective engineering and management practices and to require that these practices be followed. To ensure that these practices were understood, we sent 1,000 managers to a one-week training course. The results were extraordinary. This organization had never before delivered a product on time. Once the managers were all trained and following a disciplined planning and commitment process, the organization did not miss a single commitment for the next two and a half years.

When I retired from IBM, in 1986, I looked at the software industry in general. It was obvious that software was a crucial technology, but it was also clear that the poor state of software engineering practice seriously constrained both the U.S. economy and society in general. I made what I called an "outrageous commitment." My commitment was to transform the world of software. The objective was to bring to the world in general the practices and principles that I had found so successful at IBM.

On my retirement from IBM, I joined the Software Engineering Institute (SEI) at Carnegie Mellon University and was made director of the software process program. The SEI had just been established by the U.S. Department of Defense to improve the state of software practice. This mission was completely consistent with my "outrageous commitment," which was to get all software professionals and their managers to plan and track their work, use the best technical methods, and measure and manage the quality of this work. I was convinced that if they did, the results would be extraordinary.

Together with a small team of like-minded SEI professionals, we soon developed the Capability Maturity Model (CMM)® to

---

® Registered in the U.S. Patent and Trademark Office.

guide organizations in adopting sound management practices. The CMM has been highly effective and is used by thousands of organizations throughout the world. The CMM is now an international standard, and it is used by many branches of the U.S. government to evaluate internal software work and to assess and oversee the work of their contractors.

Although the CMM effort was and continues to be highly successful, I soon saw problems. The CMM provides excellent management guidance, but its principal impact is on the managers and their technical staffs. The CMM does not directly affect the work of the engineers, and the engineers and their teams were still struggling. There is no question that better management helps, but I soon realized that until we changed the practices of the software professionals themselves, we could never achieve a truly expert software engineering capability. Therefore, the next challenge was to motivate engineering groups to do just that. I wanted them to know the best methods, but I also wanted them to actually practice these methods every day. The techniques I developed to do this are called the Personal Software Process (PSP)[SM] and the Team Software Process (TSP)[SM]. The development of these methods is described in Chapters 6 and 7.

The story of how your organization can capitalize on these methods is told in the rest of this book. These methods are producing extraordinary results for other organizations, and you can view this as either a threat or an opportunity. As an engineering manager at Teradyne told me, "With the TSP, we're so far ahead of the competition that nobody will ever catch us."

It has been my experience that projects that use the TSP can double their productivity and improve product quality by an

---

[SM] Personal Software Process, PSP, Team Software Process, and TSP are service marks of Carnegie Mellon University.

order of magnitude. The investment required is predominantly training and mentoring costs and these costs typically are recovered within 12 to 18 months. Once teams have been trained and acquire some experience, there is no significant overhead to the TSP process. However, executive leadership is required to get your people trained properly and to support them long enough to gain the experience to practice these methods consistently.

WHY YOU SHOULD READ THIS BOOK

This book is written for senior executives who want to improve the business performance of their software groups. When I use the word *you*, I am talking to CEOs, vice presidents, and division general managers. The message of the book is designed for executives who have profit responsibility and who directly control a substantial portion of their organization's resources. As a result, much of the material has a business slant and contains a minimum of technical jargon. However, I do delve a little more deeply into the technical material than many executives might expect.

I do this for three reasons. First, executives often are suspicious of impressive presentations and like to dig a little deeper to see if there is substance behind the story. There is plenty of substance to the PSP and TSP, and I have included enough to give you a feel for the subject. Second, software is a fascinating business and you may wish to explore some elements of the subject more deeply. Third, senior and mid-level managers can use this material to guide them in improving their organization's software capability.

BOOK ORGANIZATION AND CONTENTS

In this book, I describe the software business. Whether or not you know it, you are in the software business and the performance of your software groups has a significant impact on business performance. I first describe the impact of software on your business and then review some of the most common software problems and their causes. Finally, I describe the transformation you must lead and the actions required to capitalize on the potential of software for your business.

At the end of the book, I include five appendices on installing the PSP and TSP methods and making these methods a standard part of everyday business. The sixth, and final, appendix offers a brief financial analysis of the return on investment you can expect from making these changes.

ACKNOWLEDGMENTS

First and most important, I was fortunate to receive the support and help of many people in many organizations. Among the first to help with the TSP were Iraj Hirmanpour, Tom Hilburn, and Soheil Kajenoori at Embry Riddle Aeronautical University. Their work with some early student teams was invaluable. Further, without the help of many people at many companies, the TSP could not have succeeded. In addition to those I mention elsewhere in the book, I thank Peter Bartko, John Ciurczak, Pat Ferguson, Ellen George, Steve Janiszewski, Roy Kinkaid, Bob Musson, Dan Roy, Girish Seshagiri, Rosalie Swenson, John Vu, Rich Walsh, Dave Webb, and Allen Willett for their help and support.

It is impossible to learn about engineering teams or to develop improved teamworking methods without working with actual teams. In my several years of developing the TSP, I and my associates collaborated with many helpful and perceptive software professionals and their teams. Although there is no way to thank all of these people personally, the teams provided a marvelous test bed for the early versions of the TSP process.

Developing the TSP took a lot of work, but working with these teams was the most rewarding experience of my life. To them I give my deepest thanks.

Next, I am particularly grateful to the management at the SEI for providing the opportunity to do this work. Larry Druffel, then the SEI director, kindly nominating me as an SEI fellow. This appointment allowed me to devote full time to this work. I also thank Steve Cross, Clyde Chittister, John Goodenough, Jim Over, and Bill Peterson, the current SEI management team, for their continuing encouragement and support.

When one is developing teamwork methods, it is essential to be part of a supportive and capable team. In that I was blessed with the help of Dan Burton, Noopur Davis, Marsha Pomeroy-Huff, Janice Ryan, Don McAndrews, Jim McHale, Julia Mullaney, and Jim Over. The support of my secretary, Marlene MacDonald, was invaluable, as always.

In writing books, I make a practice of asking friends and associates to review and comment on the manuscripts. For their help, I am particularly indebted to Kevin Berk, Dan Burton, David Carrington, Christine Davis, Pat Ferguson, Ellen George, Tom Hilburn, Steve Janiszewski, Soheil Khajenoori, Don McAndrews, Jim McHale, Julia Mullaney, Bob Musson, Jim Over, Bill Peterson, Marsha Pomeroy-Huff, Girish Seshagiri, Steve Shook, and Rosalie Swenson. I also much appreciate the helpful comments of my brother, professor Philip Humphrey, and of my daughter Katharine Pickman. I also thank the able staff at Addison-Wesley for their helpful and always professional support in turning my draft manuscript into this finished book.

Finally, I dedicate this book to my family. Barbara, my wife of forty-seven years, has been a marvelous companion, supporter, and constructive critic. She has also been a loving and caring mother to our seven children. Now, with six of the seven married and with nine wonderful grandchildren, our immediate family numbers twenty-four people. While I have had many jobs and countless rewarding experiences, the truly memorable times in my life have been with my family. I dedicate this book to them all.

—Watts S. Humphrey
  Sarasota, Florida

1

Every Business Is a Software Business

While technology can change quickly, getting your people to change takes a great deal longer. That is why the people-intensive job of developing software has had essentially the same problems for over 40 years. It is also why, unless you do something, the situation won't improve by itself. In fact, current trends suggest that your future products will use more software and be more complex than those of today. This means that more of your people will work on software and that their work will be harder to track and more difficult to manage. Unless you make some changes in the way your software work is done, your current problems will likely get much worse.

Regardless of the industry you are in, you almost certainly use software in just about every part of the business. For example, your software people develop and maintain the administrative systems for payroll, billing, receivables, sales tracking, and customer records. Software controls production, manages inventories, directs warehousing, and runs the distribution systems that operate your business. In service industries, your people build software to analyze, optimize, model, and support your clients. In product development, your engineers find that software is the most economical and reliable way to implement almost any sophisticated function. Software is now a critical element of computers, television sets, cell phones, and automobiles.

The quality of the software, its usability, and its timely development are critical to just about everything businesses now do. This means that, to manage your business, you must manage the software parts of that business effectively. Many managers and executives have struggled with the problem of managing software and have essentially given up. Because nothing they have tried seemed to work, they have concluded that they cannot manage software work. A common reaction is to outsource or subcontract the software work to somebody else. As many of the examples in this book show, that is often the worst possible solution. The performance of the subcontractors is generally no better, and it is often much worse.

Software work is entirely manageable, but only if you know how to manage it. The Software Engineering Institute (SEI) at Carnegie Mellon University was established by the U.S. Department of Defense in 1984 to work on the software problem. Its people have been addressing this problem ever since. They have learned why software work is so troublesome and what you can do about it. They have packaged their findings in a family of methods that are designed to help businesses like yours. This chapter summarizes the principles of this work, and the rest of the book describes what you can do to apply these principles to your organization.

THE PRINCIPLES OF SOFTWARE MANAGEMENT

To manage a software-intensive business, you must observe three management principles.

Principle Number One: Recognize That You Are in the Software Business

Whether or not you know it, you are almost certainly in the software business. If yours is like most businesses, software plays a pivotal role in most of your operations. For example, software schedule delays affect product delivery dates, and product delivery dates drive cost, revenue, and profit. Unless you can manage revenue and profit, you cannot manage a business. If you do not treat software as a critical part of your future, you cannot manage software, and then you might not even be able to manage your business.

Principle Number Two: Quality Must Be *the* Top Priority

In software work, quality problems overwhelm everything else. Quality is critical, and when quality is not managed, entire software projects are unmanageable. There are known ways to manage software quality, but they require proper training and disciplined engineering methods. The key need is for you to make a commitment to quality. You must make software quality *the* top priority.

Principle Number Three: Quality Software Is Developed by Disciplined and Motivated People

You cannot run an effective software operation without disciplined and motivated people. Software development is intellectual work, and undisciplined or unmotivated people cannot do timely or predictable intellectual work. Your people must be personally committed to their work, and they must care about the quality of the products they produce. Quality work is not done by accident; it is done only by skilled and motivated people.

These are the basic principles for managing software work. While they may seem obvious, they are not simple. As the examples in the rest of this chapter show, if you fail to follow any one of these principles, you cannot have a productive or effective software operation.

WHY EVERY BUSINESS IS A SOFTWARE BUSINESS

A senior vice president of Citibank once told me that "we are a software business masquerading as a bank." He explained that they could not run the bank without software. I see this situation in business after business: software is now a critical part of running many businesses. Some executives recognize it, but many others do not.

One example of the growth of software is in weapon systems. Figure 1.1 shows the growth of software in military aircraft from 1960 to 2000. With the F-4 in 1960, software supported only 8% of the functions the pilot performed. With the F-16 in 1982, this proportion had reached 45% and, with the newest F-22 in 2000, software controls 80% of everything the pilot does [1]. As

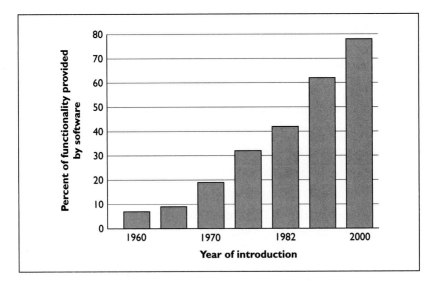

Figure 1.1 Software functionality in military aircraft

one general said, "The only thing you can do with an F-22 that does not require software is take a picture of it." That, of course, assumes that you are not using a digital camera.

The speed with which your people develop software can put you ahead of or behind your competitors. Software problems may have been frustrating in the past, but mismanaged software can now be fatal to a business. If your people do not produce quality software, testing times will be excessive, schedules will slip, and revenue will drop. You could soon be in serious trouble. The consequences of these problems are predictable.

1. If you extend schedules to make realistic customer commitments, you lose business.

2. If you make competitive commitments, your software is late and your customers are unhappy.

3. If you do this too often, you will be known as an unreliable supplier and have unhappy and disloyal customers.

4. If this condition continues for long, you will lose so many customers that you could well go out of business.

Even Fortune 500 businesses can fail, and often very quickly. In this fast-paced world, you rarely get a second chance—you must do the job right the first time. There is no second prize and no time to learn from mistakes. In fact, you rarely have time to catch up. Then, if you are not competitive, the business consequences will likely be severe.

WE'RE IN THE *HARDWARE* BUSINESS

IBM management did not understand the first principle of software management: they were in the software business. The consequences were severe. For many years, IBM thought of itself as a hardware company. It had started manufacturing and selling punched-card machines. It wasn't until the 1960s that IBM got into the computer business in a big way. Even then, IBM's senior management had grown up in the punched-card era and could not see the potential of software. They viewed software as an expense and thought they could make money only with hardware.

In 1976, the IBM CEO recognized that the personal computer (PC) business was important. He also found that engineering had no PC products under development or even planned. He pushed the development divisions for several years but finally lost his patience. Then he set up a special PC project that reported directly to him. He told this group to get a product on the market within a year.

The PC engineering group was formed quickly, and the product manager was told to break any IBM traditions that got in the way. IBM had recently disbanded its centralized programming group, and each hardware product team had software people of its own. Since the PC group was newly formed, it had no software resources and there was no centralized programming department from which to obtain help. The PC product manager had to get his programming support from a young entrepreneur named Bill Gates, who was just starting a company called Microsoft.

IBM announced the PC about a year later, and it was an enormous success. The company expanded production and extended marketing throughout the world. As PC demand grew, they added new models and enhanced performance and capacity. At the same time, Microsoft was enhancing the PC software.

When the PC was introduced, IBM was the third most profitable company in the world, and Microsoft was not even ranked among the top industrial organizations. Within ten years, IBM had the largest operating loss in history. Over the same period,

Microsoft had grown spectacularly and had a market valuation more than twice that of IBM. It took another ten years, a complete change of management, and a downsizing of 200,000 employees for IBM to address the new software-intensive marketplace.

MAINTAIN CONTROL OF PRODUCT UNIQUENESS

IBM forgot a key business tenet: identify and protect that kernel that makes your products and services unique. Why did people want a PC? They did not want simply to have a pretty box. They wanted to do something, often something that no one had imagined. The power of computers is their flexibility, and the PC put this flexibility in the hands of the public. This flexibility was due entirely to the software.

When IBM realized that ceding control over the PC software to Microsoft was a mistake, it sank many millions into developing the OS/2 software system. OS/2 was an excellent system, but it was too late. Microsoft was too far ahead and the PC software business was moving too fast. IBM could not catch up.

IBM did not realize that the uniqueness of the PC product was in what it could do, and what it could do was almost entirely determined by the software. IBM got no software revenue from the PCs it sold, and the hardware soon became a low-profit commodity. The real tragedy is that IBM is no longer even a major force in the PC hardware business. That is now a commodity business, and whoever controls the PC software controls the PC business. Today, that is Microsoft, not IBM.

The Lesson of Principle Number One

With modern sophisticated products, the unique functions are increasingly embodied in the software, and a product's uniqueness is what makes it profitable. Therefore, if you do not recognize that you are in the software business and do not own the software in your products and services, you will lose control of your product's uniqueness. Then you will likely lose control of business revenue and profit.

QUALITY IS MORE IMPORTANT THAN SCHEDULE

Ashton Tate did not appreciate software management principle number two: that software quality must be the top priority. Their experiences illustrate the dangers of this mistake. The Ashton Tate business started in 1980 with the introduction of the Dbase database management program. This program was soon the market leader, and Ashton Tate was one of the software industry's big three. In 1987, Ashton Tate had sales of $215 million, only slightly behind Lotus at $283 million and Microsoft at $260 million. The Dbase product accounted for 65% of Ashton Tate's business.

When competitors started offering faster and easier-to-use database products, Ashton Tate developed an enhanced version called Dbase IV. In February 1988, it announced that Dbase IV would ship in May. In May, it announced a delay of two months, and in August it announced another two-month delay. In late September, Ashton Tate announced that the new Dbase product would ship by the end of October, when it was finally sent off to customers.

Unfortunately, Dbase IV had so many defects that, after it had been used for a few months, Ashton Tate had to withdraw it. In September 1989, when I met with Ashton Tate's CEO, the engineers were still testing and fixing Dbase IV. When the CEO asked for suggestions, I asked if he had any data on the product's quality problems. My suggestion was to look at these defect data and identify the most troublesome of the system's modules, or parts. Then they could focus on repairing the most defective modules. Since software defects typically cluster in a small percentage of the modules, Aston Tate's engineers could clean up most of the problems in about four months. However, because the CEO was committed to ship Dbase IV in two months, he did not follow my advice.

The Ashton Tate engineers continued testing Dbase IV, and they kept finding and fixing more defects. They did not ship in two months, and they were still testing and fixing problems a year later. By February 1991, Dbase IV was still in beta test and the CEO was replaced. Because of its quality problems, Ashton Tate reported a $5.6 million quarterly loss. It was soon bought by Borland. Ashton Tate, once the third largest company in the software industry, no longer exists.

The root cause of this problem was poor quality management. Ashton Tate had announced its Dbase IV product in February 1988 for delivery in May. The schedule kept slipping until finally, in October 1988, management said, "Ship it; we'll fix it later." This converted a schedule problem into a quality disaster. Instead of being late and inconveniencing their customers, they were now betting the company. Sadly, they lost the bet.

The Lesson of Principle Number Two

Ashton Tate's engineers and managers viewed software quality as a testing problem. As described later in this book, there are better ways to manage quality. However, these better ways all start with you. If you do not insist on quality from the very beginning, people will rush through their work, expecting somebody else to fix it later. Testing is enormously expensive, often taking half of the software development schedule. By using proven quality methods, these costs can be cut by ten or more times and schedules accelerated by many months or even years. Teradyne, in just two years, saved $5.3 million. That is why quality is important, and that is why you must make it the top priority. Everybody else can defer quality problems, but you must live with the consequences. Quality is an economic choice: pay a little now or a fortune later.

Another important lesson from the Ashton Tate experience concerns time-to-market. Most businesses quickly learn the importance of getting a product into the market at the right time. However, many make the assumption that time-to-market and quality are mutually exclusive. If you must get to market quickly, they reason, you will have to skimp on quality and ram products out fast as you can. As the Ashton Tate experience shows, this quick-and-dirty strategy is often slow and very expensive. To truly accelerate development work and optimize time-to-market, your people must do their jobs the right way the very first time. This reduces testing time and minimizes rework. Accomplishing this requires a corporate commitment to quality.

IN SOFTWARE, WHAT MUST HAPPEN OFTEN DOES NOT

The next example illustrates what can happen when managers do not follow software principle number three: that quality software is developed by disciplined and motivated people. I met Larry, the vice president of engineering, when his group was developing a large integrated production control system. Software delivery was committed for the following September, and it was only April, so Larry was optimistic that they would make it. He wanted my opinion.

When I asked about status, Larry explained that the coding was almost finished and that integration and system testing were under way. However, when I asked about product data, he did not know what I meant. I told him that, to understand where they stood, I had to know the size of the planned product, how much code had been written to date, how much had been released to integration and system test, and when it was released. He did not have this information.

Before giving Larry my opinion, I talked to the key managers and several of the engineers on the project. I also talked to the testers. Then I told Larry my conclusions. The system was just now starting testing and, based on the quality practices I had observed, the job was only about half done. Since the company had been developing this system for over a year, there was at least a year to go. While the product might be shipped in September, it would be in September of the following year.

Larry refused to believe me. They had to ship *this* September. While it was true that the business desperately needed an earlier shipment, they didn't even ship a year later. The company eventually ran out of money and was sold to a competitor. This is a classic case of poor software management.

The Lesson of Principle Number Three

Software managers and professionals who are not trained in quality methods will not believe that quality is important and will not follow the disciplined practices required to build quality products. Then testing will take at least half of the development schedule. Until you overcome this poor quality attitude, your people will not follow disciplined quality practices, and you cannot get quality software. Every aspect of software must start with quality, even the engineers' attitudes.

A QUALITY COMMITMENT

While few people talk about quality, and while software projects rarely have quality goals, most people would agree, "Of course, we must produce a quality product." Quality work is not an accident. People must believe that quality is important, and they must strive to produce quality products. Quality is like any other part of your business: if you don't measure it, you can't manage it, and if you don't manage it, it will not improve. Software quality can be measured, but until engineers measure and manage the quality of their work, the quality of their work will not improve.

No other modern technology rushes products through design and implementation and fixes them in test. Semiconductor engineers know that quality is critical. They cannot test and fix chips at the end of the line. When Toyota embraced the quality teachings of Dr. W. E. Deming, they demonstrated to Detroit that by managing quality, they could produce better cars and save money [2]. Finding and fixing problems in test is expensive for semiconductors, for automobiles, and for software.

Why don't software engineers focus on quality? It's not because they are lazy or unmotivated, but because of the way they have been trained and managed. Starting with their first programming courses, engineers learn that the most admired programmers produce code at lightning speed. Then they find and fix the defects in test. This fix-it-later attitude fosters poor practices throughout the software process. There are no quality standards, design standards, or even much in the way of implementation standards. To get quality work, you must change this culture.

If all engineers are poorly trained and if they all do undisciplined work, what can you do? Since you can't afford unpredictable schedules and poor-quality products, you must make changes in the way software is developed. The key questions are the following:

- Is there a better way to manage software?
- Is this better way economical?
- Is there a practical way to change organizations so they will consistently follow sound and high-quality engineering methods?

The answers are yes, yes, and yes. In the rest of this book I discuss ways to introduce effective software quality and management practices. The methods I describe—the Personal Software Process (PSP) and the Team Software Process (TSP)^{SM}—are also attractive financially. As shown in Chapter 8 and Appendix F, an investment in these methods will yield a return of over 300%. Finally, a defined and available introduction program is available to help you and your people adopt these methods.

SUMMARY AND CONCLUSIONS

The following five principal points are made in this chapter:

1. Software is increasingly important to your business. If you can't effectively manage your software work, you will have trouble managing anything else.

2. The first principle of software management is to recognize that you are in the software business and to treat software management as critical.

3. The second principle of software management is that quality comes first, even before the schedule.

4. The third principle of software management is that, to consistently produce quality software, you must have disciplined and motivated professional teams.

5. There are known ways to manage software, but you must know them and you must use them. This book explains these methods, how to introduce them, and how to use them.

---

^{SM} Personal Software Process, PSP, Team Software Process, and TSP are service marks of Carnegie Mellon University.

Although sound software practices are not difficult, they are not obvious. The PSP and TSP provide an overall framework to guide engineers, managers, and executives through building and running an effective and productive software business.

REFERENCES

1. Jack Ferguson. "Crouching Dragon, Hidden Software: Software in DoD Weapon Systems." *IEEE Software* (July/August 2001), pp. 105–107.

2. W. Edwards Deming, *Out of the Crisis.* Cambridge, MA: MIT Center for Advanced Engineering Study, 1982.

2
Why Projects Fail

Although there are many ways to define project failure, the Standish Group reports that over 50% of software projects are either canceled or over 100% late [1]. These projects could almost certainly be classed as failures, at least in business terms. Managers are often surprised to learn that software projects rarely fail for technical reasons; invariably, the problem is poor management. Technical problems often exist, but they are rarely decisive. The ways to mismanage software projects are many, but proper management requires only two things: a dedication to quality and motivated engineers who do disciplined software work. In software, managers generally concentrate on getting the work done and pay little or no attention to *how* this work is done. As the cases in this chapter show, the principal cause of project failure is inadequate attention to the disciplines with which the work is done.

THE CRASH PROJECT THAT ALMOST CRASHED

Angie was a project manager at a large financial services company. She had just been given a new job and would soon turn over her current project to the lead engineer. She asked for my views on her new job. This project had all the hallmarks of a disaster. Barry, the vice president for business strategy, had reviewed all of the company's products and seen an opportunity for a new Internet financial service. Because no one else then offered this service, he wanted a new product in a hurry. Barry then met with the CEO, who liked the idea, and they agreed on a September goal for launching the new offering. It was only January, so this eight-month schedule seemed reasonable to them.

When Barry talked to engineering, he found that almost everyone was committed to other jobs and that only three people could be assigned to this project. Since Barry was now committed to the CEO for the September date, he told engineering to hire a software subcontracting firm to staff the work. Barry and the engineering VP then drew up a project schedule that met the September delivery date and told the engineers to get started.

After several months of work, the CEO asked for a project review. Angie was on the review team, and she found that the project plan was totally unrealistic. In trying to meet the September date, the engineers had rushed through the design so the subcontractors could start coding. Lots of code was being written, but there was no system specification and the component interfaces were not even defined. Angie felt that a major redesign would be required. She also found that the lack of a detailed plan meant that no one knew where the project stood. The few management milestones gave the engineers no guidance, and they were blindly plowing ahead with the coding in hope that they could somehow make the system work in test.

Angie knew that, unless she made major changes, this project would fail. It had an unrealistic schedule, there were not enough engineers, the objectives had not been written, and the programmers were slapping out code to meet the CEO's date. Most of the contractor's work was useless and she had to build a new engineering team, produce an overall design, and start over on the implementation. While she recognized the problems in time and was able to make a realistic plan, she had to slip the delivery date to the following May.

THE CAUSES OF PROJECT FAILURE

When you want a project in the worst way, that is often the way you get it. A crash effort to meet a seemingly impossible schedule is often a total loss. Two questions have often bothered me about software work. First, why do competent software professionals agree to dates when they have no idea how to meet them? Second, why do rational executives accept schedule commitments when the engineers offer no evidence that they can meet these commitments? Where software is concerned, many otherwise hardheaded executives willingly accept vague promises and incomplete plans. An uncritical or illogical approach to software commitments is a common element of software project failure. As you will see, management's undisciplined approach to commitments contributes to every one of the five most common causes of project failure:

1. Unrealistic schedules

2. Inappropriate staffing

3. Changing requirements

4. Poor quality work

5. Believing in magic

Unrealistic Schedules

You might think that pushing for an aggressive schedule would accelerate the work, but it actually delays it. When faced with an unrealistic schedule, engineering teams often behave irrationally.

They race through the requirements, produce a superficial design, and rush into coding. This mad scramble to build something—anything—generally ends up with a poor-quality product that has the wrong functions, is seriously defective, and is late. When software projects start with unrealistic schedules, they are invariably delivered much later than they would have been with a rational plan. These are the typical results when quality is not managed, engineering teams use undisciplined methods, and executives make commitments without plans to support them. Angie's project is a good example of what can happen in such situations.

Inappropriate Staffing

The only way to complete an engineering project rapidly and efficiently is to assign an adequate number of people and then protect them from interruptions and distractions. This helps build the motivation and effective teamwork needed for quality results. When management fails to provide timely, adequate, and properly trained resources, their projects generally will fail.

Sandy's project was developing the control software for a large transportation system. The work was started in time and the engineers had what appeared to be a realistic schedule. However, I later learned that most of the engineers were simultaneously assigned to several jobs and that management staffed projects only when they became crises. Not only were the engineers unable to spend much time on any one project, they felt that none of their jobs was important. When a project was really important, management dedicated engineers to that job. The typical engineering reaction to a part-time assignment was this: "If management isn't committed to the job, why should I be?"

Sandy was the only engineer on her project with a full-time assignment. Everybody else had at least one other project assignment and several had two. The team made modest progress for about two months until Sandy got pulled off for another crisis. Then everything fell apart. Since nobody but Sandy seemed to care if the work was done, nobody else spent time on the job after she left.

This staffing problem was caused by Rich, the company president. He stayed personally in touch with every major customer and was involved whenever problems arose. When a customer complained that a project was behind schedule, Rich would call the lab and get more engineers assigned. This meant that projects were always understaffed until they became crises, and then they would be fully staffed. One could argue that, because they were eventually completed, these projects did not fail. However they were all late and over budget and the company was losing money. In any rational business sense, these projects were failures. The cause was the lack of a disciplined and motivating engineering environment, which in turn was caused by Rich's undisciplined way of managing commitments.

Changing Requirements During Development

To start designing and building products, engineers must know what product to build. Unfortunately, management, marketing, and even customers often don't know what they want. What is often worse, they think they know and then change their minds partway through the job. While the requirements (or objectives) normally change during the early phases of a job, there is a point beyond which changes are damaging. After this point, changes waste time and money and disrupt the work.

My very first large software project at IBM taught me an indelible lesson about changing requirements. While IBM was developing its 360 system, MIT research work on time-sharing found that a new memory feature, known as virtual memory, was necessary.* MIT tried to convince IBM to include virtual memory in its 360 system design. However, the 360 designers did not agree with the need and felt that few customers would want it. MIT then formed a joint development project with GE, an IBM competitor, to develop virtual memory time-sharing for a planned new GE computer.

The proposed GE Multics System attracted considerable interest from important IBM customers. IBM marketing reported that Lincoln Laboratory, Bell Telephone Laboratories, and several leading universities were about to order time-sharing systems from GE. They also said that the new GE system was being considered by most of IBM's important accounts. Management asked me to form a new marketing and engineering group to develop an IBM time-sharing system to meet this threat. I assembled a talented team of developers who devised an enhanced model of the 360 line that included virtual memory. We called this new system the TSS/67. Lincoln Laboratory and Bell Telephone Laboratories both ordered this new system, and we quickly got many other orders.

A few months later General Motors, IBM's largest and most important customer, asked IBM and GE for proposals for time-sharing systems. General Motors planned to use this system for a new graphics design application and needed an enhanced version of virtual memory to handle the massive memory required. The GE/MIT team had agreed to include the General Motors-requested feature, but our engineers objected. They said that the design of the TSS/67 system was past the point where they could make such a change without major rework.

---

* Time-sharing was the early name for systems with multiple remote user terminals. Almost all large computing systems built today use time-sharing.

Marketing said that if we did not include this General Motors feature, we would lose this order and many others, including the one we had already won from Bell Labs. This seemed like too big a risk to me, so I agreed with marketing. I told the engineers to add the expanded virtual memory feature, and we negotiated a three-month schedule extension with the existing customers. We then won the General Motors and University of Michigan orders. Now the big challenge was to deliver.

Although this sounds like a great success, it turned into a disaster. The engineers worked valiantly, but they could not meet the new schedule. I soon realized that the changes we had made to win the General Motors order were much more extensive than I had expected. The system was six months late getting into test and had serious performance problems. As testing continued, most of the TSS/67 customers switched to the standard 360 systems and the TSS/67 system missed its window of opportunity. A few TSS/67 systems were installed, but IBM ultimately withdrew it and later incorporated virtual memory into the company's standard computer line. The TSS/67 debacle cost IBM about $30 million and was a market failure. Development of the GE Multics system also took much longer than planned, and it too was a business and marketing failure.

While the requirements change might seem to be the source of the problem, it was only the catalyst. The real problem was that I did not observe the third principle of software management: to use disciplined and motivated professionals. To truly follow that principle, I should not have committed the team to a date they did not believe in.

Requirements changes are never easy, and committing to such changes without a detailed plan to do the work is always a mistake. Even more important, the engineers who will do the work must make the plan and agree with the resulting schedule. Only then will you have a truly motivated team.

Poor-Quality Work

Six engineers at a consumer electronics company were developing a major enhancement for the company's manufacturing control system. This enhancement was needed to support a new production system that would be both more efficient and faster than the current line. The manufacturing VP wanted to accelerate the work, but the project manager argued that the current schedule was already the best the team could do. When the laboratory director took this position upstairs, the engineering VP told him to get a new project manager who would meet the desired date.

Greg, the new project manager, agreed to the manufacturing VP's date and unmercifully pushed his engineers. They rushed through the design and coding, skipped all of the quality reviews and inspections, and got into test in record time. Testing found many defects, and Greg argued with the testing department about every one, insisting that most of the defects were problems the factory would never see. He also argued that testing was running too many tests. When the first tests ran, engineering should ship the product. They could fix the remaining defects later. Greg won his argument, and the system was installed in the factory on the desired schedule.

Since Greg met the manufacturing VP's date, one could argue that he was a hero. However, the system was a disaster. It was so unreliable that the engineers had to make fixes every time the production mix or product parameters changed. When the quality manager reviewed the program, he found that the excessive factory downtime and the unplanned engineering support had cost the company over $1,000,000.

Problems often come in pairs. When executives push for unrealistic schedules, the project either will be late in delivering a working product or will produce a product that doesn't work. There is a saying about software quality: If it doesn't have to work, we can build it really fast. Here, both Greg and the engineering VP failed to follow two of the principles of software management: a dedication to quality and building a motivated and disciplined working environment.

Believing in Magic

COTS, or commercial-off-the-shelf software, is an attractive way to save development time and money. It seems like a waste of engineering effort to develop products when the same or similar products are already available elsewhere. As Roger found out, however, COTS is not a silver bullet. If not properly managed, it can be a disaster.

Roger had a crash project to introduce a new insurance agency product, but he could not fully staff his project to meet the desired schedule. He had four engineers on board, but the other eight would not be available for at least three months. To reduce the amount of work to something his four engineers could handle, Roger found an existing COTS product they could use as a base. This would eliminate much of their development work.

This COTS product was the central control portion of a custom-developed insurance system. Since it provided most of the functions Roger's applications needed, this looked like an ideal solution. Roger's team could complete their first application in time, and the software company that owned the COTS product promised to make the required changes in three months. However, the company would work only under a time-and-materials contract.

Roger signed a contract for delivery of the modified COTS product in three months. His four engineers developed the first of the new applications on time and planned to develop the others over three subsequent releases. This seemed like a great success. The contractor delivered within the promised three months and the first application package was available on time. However, testing was a nightmare. Even though the COTS product worked perfectly in demonstrations, every time the testers stressed the system with different hardware configurations, higher data rates, or even data entry errors, the system would crash. In the end, testing took almost four months longer than expected and the COTS work cost almost twice what was planned.

The lesson of this story is that it generally costs as much to test and fix a defective product as it took to develop it in the first place. While Roger was in a hurry and didn't have engineers when he needed them, the poor quality of this COTS product cost him four additional months and a lot of money.

Everyone would like to start with a quality product, but you cannot simply look at a program to determine its quality. You must test it, and test it thoroughly enough to expose previously untested conditions. If the program is troublesome when stressed, it will almost certainly be troublesome when used. Stress testing takes time, however, and Roger didn't have time.

Although you can't easily tell the quality of a program, you can ask if it was properly developed. The principle here is that if the engineers used a quality process to develop the product, you would almost certainly have a quality product. However, to determine the quality of a process, you must know what a quality process looks like and you must know that the engineers followed that process with the discipline required to produce a quality product. As we shall see in later chapters, asking and answering this question is the key to managing software work.

THE EXECUTIVE ROLE IN PROJECT FAILURE

The preceding five examples show the problems caused by poor software management. In Angie's case, the schedule was so aggressive that management panicked and started without a competent plan or even a sound technical strategy. While the CEO had not intended to set an unreasonable date, he knew that relaxed goals get relaxed results. He believed that energetic work came only from aggressive goals. This is a common executive attitude, but it is too simplistic. He should also have insisted that the engineers produce a detailed plan for the job.

On Sandy's project, neither Rich nor the other managers set priorities. When engineers have several simultaneous assignments, management is in effect telling them, "We have all this work and don't know how to do it. You figure it out." Needless to say, this approach doesn't work. For engineers to be motivated and productive, management must decide which jobs are important and then assign the needed staff to do them. When managers don't do this, the projects will almost certainly fail. Rich and his senior managers should have established project priorities, fully staffed the most important projects, and established recovery plans for the others.

In the TSS/67 case, I was the executive, and I had a tough problem. IBM had not anticipated a key market need, and we had to do something. While my decision was understandable, it was unwise. With more experience, I should have realized that what General Motors wanted was more than either GE or IBM could do. The change was simply too big and too late. If we had stuck to the initial plan and then enhanced the system after the first version was working, we would have been the first to have a working system. Then, even if GE had won the General Motors order, we would have ended up with the installation. My mistake was in making a snap decision and not having the discipline to first get a detailed plan for the work. When your engineers tell you that a schedule is impossible, it probably is.

Greg's story is a classic case of the hot-shot manager who is brought in to save the battle but loses the war. For most projects, the need is for a working product, not a responsive promise.

When someone promises to deliver on your desired date, watch out. The product might not work. The cost of poor quality is rarely visible until the end of the project. Often, in fact, the poor-quality product will continue causing customer problems long after the project is over. The costs of poor quality continue for a very long time.

Roger's case shows how an unquestioning belief in a miraculous answer can lead to serious problems. If a solution looks too good to be true, it probably is. While using COTS products, subcontracting parts of a job, or outsourcing an entire project can be effective, that depends on the quality of the resulting product. If you don't manage quality, you probably won't get it.

These five examples describe seemingly different problems but they have two errors in common: managers made undisciplined commitments, and they did not insist that the job be done properly. Unrealistic schedules, inappropriate staffing, disruptive requirements changes, and poor-quality products are all results of undisciplined work, either by the engineers or by their managers. The only way to consistently prevent project failures is to insist that everyone do quality work. Chapters 5 through 8 describe how to temper aggressive goals with realistic planning and quality management.

Once you are in the software business, you must follow the other two principles of software management. Quality must be the top priority, and disciplined work is essential.

SUMMARY AND CONCLUSIONS

The following three principal points are made in this chapter:

1. The two key components of software management are a dedication to quality and consistently disciplined engineering work.

2. When software projects fail, it is usually because a manager did not insist that the work be done in the right way.

3. The five most common causes of project failure are unrealistic schedules, inappropriate staffing, disruptive requirements changes, poor-quality work, and believing in magic. All of these problems could have been avoided had management insisted on planned and disciplined work.

REFERENCE

1. Jim Johnson, "Chaos: The Dollar Drain of IT Project Failures." *Application Development Trends* (January 1995), pp. 41–47.

3

Rational Management

In Chapter 1, I described the three principles of software management: recognizing that you are in the software business, making quality the first priority, and using motivated and disciplined people to do the work. Then, in Chapter 2, we reviewed five of the principal causes of project failure: unrealistic schedules, inappropriate staffing, disruptive requirements changes, poor-quality work, and believing in magic. Now, in this chapter, we discuss solutions to these problems. As H. L. Mencken once said, "For every complex problem, there is a simple answer, and it's wrong." While there is no single solution to software's multiple problems, there is an effective strategy. It concerns management style and the techniques for enlisting your people in attacking the problems of your business. I call this style rational management. The principle of rational management is that your people are loyal and thinking professionals who would like to support you in addressing the organization's problems.

FACING FACTS

When faced with a software problem, many executives behave irrationally. As we saw in Chapter 1, the Ashton Tate CEO knew that he had to ship Dbase IV in November, so that's what he told his management team. Not surprisingly, they said they could do it. However, any rational examination of the situation would have shown that, by just continuing to test and fix defects, they didn't have a chance. So what would a rational manager do instead?

When you are in an impossible situation, gather the available facts, assess these facts to understand the problems, and then rationally address these problems. After all, if the situation looks truly impossible, it probably is; then pushing ahead and hoping for a miracle will only make matters worse. Rational management means making plans, following these plans, and fixing problems before they get out of control. It requires that you trust your people, be honest with your customers, and insist on professional work. The stories in this chapter give examples of how this rational approach can help you to resolve issues and to take advantage of business opportunities. While rational management isn't easy, it does work.

CUTTING CYCLE TIME

Cycle time is rarely defined precisely, yet most organizations consider it their most important competitive yardstick. Cycle time refers to the time from project inception to the first product offering to customers. If you don't measure cycle time, you cannot manage it, and if you don't manage cycle time, it almost certainly won't improve. The following story shows how many organizations manage cycle time.

I was in India for a conference and took the opportunity to visit the Bangalore laboratory of a company I was working with. My first meeting was with the laboratory director. He explained that corporate headquarters had established this laboratory as a test bed for improved software methods. He also explained that the CEO had just challenged all the product groups to improve cycle time by ten times in ten years. This number seemed so extraordinary that I asked the lab director for more details. He assured me that the CEO was serious and that they really were trying to shorten the typical two-year project to a two-and-a-half-month job.

I spent the next three days meeting with project leaders and engineers. I held several informal 90-minute sessions with groups of about 10 to 15 engineers each. After a few opening comments, I would ask each engineer to explain his or her job and to discuss any important issues or problems. In three days of meetings, not one engineer mentioned cycle time. While management was clearly concerned about the cycle-time goal, nobody was doing anything about it. I concluded that the managers had no idea how to achieve the goal, so they did not know what to tell the engineers. Not surprisingly, the goal was ignored and cycle time was not improved. Today, one of that company's biggest problems is its inability to bring new products to market as quickly as its competitors. Instead of cycle time improving by ten times, it actually got worse.

Aggressive goals can be useful, but they are useful only if they lead to productive action. That usually requires that people change their behavior. This, in turn, requires an improvement plan that focuses on achievable goals and on the actions needed to achieve them. While a ten-times cycle-time improvement in ten years may not be achievable, the same goal could have been broken into ten annual improvements of 25% each. A one-year goal to improve cycle time by 25% would probably seem reasonable. It might even be achievable, as long as the goal was measured and tracked and the work was supported by a detailed improvement plan.

The first element of rational management is a direct outgrowth of the principles of software management. To get motivated and disciplined people, you need aggressive goals and you need to support these goals with specific programs and plans to achieve them. Most important, reduce any long-term goals to short-term actions with checkpoints and measures. Then measure these goals and use the measures to track and manage the work.

YOU'RE RUINING THE BUSINESS

IBM had just fired the director of programming. The senior vice president had called a meeting with the senior programming management team. He was so mad that he was pounding the table. The company had announced a complete new line of computers a year and a half before. IBM was now delivering the hardware, but the OS/360 programming support had slipped three times. The problem for the business was that customers were delaying their computer orders until they had believable dates for the software. The VP ended his tirade by telling us we were ruining the business. Then he demanded that we give him a schedule in two weeks. No one said a word. Everybody in the room looked at me.

I had just been named director of programming, and I knew that two weeks was insane. I had nearly 4,000 programmers in 15 laboratories and 7 countries. Most of them were working on the OS/360 system. This was a major corporate crisis, but I knew that any schedule guess would almost certainly be wrong. If I made up a date and missed it, my credibility would be gone; then I, too, would be out of a job. I told the VP that I could give him a date that day if he insisted but we'd probably have another date tomorrow. If he wanted a responsible date, we would have to make a plan. That would take 60 days. The VP looked around the room. One by one, he asked all the managers what they thought. They all agreed that it would take 60 days. In the end, he agreed to the 60 days.

When executives tell me they are in a crisis and don't have time to do the job properly, I tell them that when they are really in a crisis, they cannot afford to panic. A crisis is no time to wing it. Since the time wasted to recover from mistakes would only make things worse, you must do the job in the very best way you can. You must make complete plans and review these plans to ensure that they are realistic and sound. After all, if your job depends on meeting the plan, you had better have a good plan. By facing the facts, we did solve the OS/360 problem. While we delayed the schedules, this team produced a plan everyone understood and believed in, and they did it in the promised 60 days. What is more, they did not miss a single date for the next two and a half years.

The second element of rational management is planning. This again connects to our principles for managing software. For truly motivated people, you need aggressive goals and plans, but your people must also believe in the plans and be committed to meet them. So the second element of rational management is to insist on plans, and insist that these plans be made by the people who will do the work. Then review the plans to make sure they are complete, they are based on data, and you are willing to bet your job on meeting the planned dates. Finally, make sure all of the people involved are committed to meeting these plans. If they say they can't meet your date, believe them. The chances of your getting an earlier schedule are nil. By negotiating the plan with the people who will do the work, you give them a stake in the job and you ensure that they are all committed to meeting that schedule.

GETTING THE FACTS

Crises are common in software, and they commonly cause panic. Whether the problem is with hardware or software, a good rule to follow in a crisis is this: get the facts. A search for facts is a great way to avoid panic. Ask questions and demand answers. If you don't get good answers, the engineers probably don't know them. But, by asking some questions, you can almost always find some useful data. Be persistent and continue to probe. When you obtain all of the available facts, then you can devise the fastest and most effective way to solve the problem. The next story provides a good example of how facts and data can help a business.

Frank was president of a small company that made communications switching equipment. The company's profit margin was eroding, and customer complaints were increasing. Warranty and field support costs were way over budget, and most of the engineers were fixing customer problems instead of developing new products. The company had shipped its newest product three years before and, although it worked well, the users kept finding problems. As they added new users, these users found even more problems.

Frank wanted my advice. When I asked for details, however, he didn't have any facts. To understand the problem, I told him that we had to know how many defects had been found, how these defects were distributed among the system's modules (or parts), and what it cost to fix each defect. Without these data, there was no way to make a logical decision on how to address his problems.

Neither Frank nor his managers thought anyone had the data we needed. However, we soon found a maintenance engineer who did. He had gathered data from defect reports and we were able to piece together the needed information. Figure 3.1 shows what we found. The company had repaired a total of 686 defects in the first three years of customer use. The system had 1,643 modules, but 81% of them had been defect-free. All of the defects had been found in only 19% of the modules, and only 4% of the modules accounted for 48% of the defects.

These data showed that nearly half of the company's maintenance costs were due to only 4% of the system's modules. With

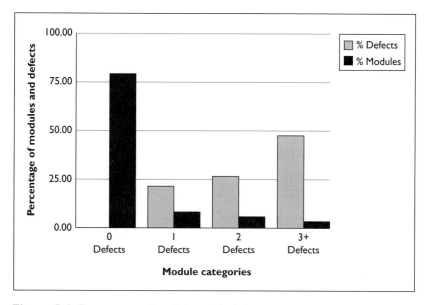

Figure 3.1 Percentage of modules with defects

this information, it took the engineers only five months to clean up the 72 defective modules. This cut maintenance costs in half. By the end of the year, the company's profit margin was back where it belonged.

The third element of rational management is to use facts and data. This again connects to the principles of software management. With motivated and disciplined teams, your people will know how and why to gather data, and they will consistently measure their work and report the results. By objectively using the team's facts and data, you demonstrate trust in your people and a willingness to listen to their problems, plans, and ideas.

Once you have engineers who do quality work and who have the discipline to consistently do such work, you can set realistic and aggressive goals, make sound decisions, and precisely track the work. Often, as the next story shows, a little data can help to resolve problems before they impact the business.

THE FLIGHT-TEST DEADLINE

When Bret launched his project in October, he knew that the U.S. Air Force needed the completed system by the end of December in the following year. This was a major avionics upgrade to support a critical January flight test, only 15 months hence. Since Bret's team was using the Team Software Process (TSP), the engineers had detailed plans that showed them what to do each week.

After the first six weeks of work, the team's weekly progress reports showed that they were falling behind. As illustrated in Figure 3.2, their earned-value (EV)* projection showed that they were slipping schedule by about 8% a week. While this

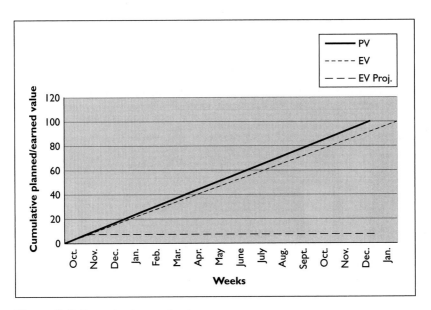

Figure 3.2 Earned-value projection

---

* Earned value measures a team's progress against its plan. Each task's planned value (PV) equals that task's planned percentage of the total job. When that task is completed, the project earns that value (EV). By projecting EV progress, teams can accurately predict when they will finish.

might seem like a small problem, it was enough to miss the December delivery by over a month. Bret waited until after the Thanksgiving and Christmas holidays, but then he asked the entire team to go on overtime.

By working six-day weeks for the next three months, the team caught up. Thereafter, Bret and the team reviewed progress every week. If some engineers fell behind in one week, they had to make up the shortfall the next week or go on overtime. Because the engineers could precisely track progress, they finished the project slightly ahead of schedule, with only a little additional overtime.

The fourth element of rational management is to use facts and data to anticipate and correct problems before they become disasters. An 8% correction is only about three hours a week, but if you wait a year, it grows to a full month. Schedules slip a day at a time, and if your project measures cannot detect a one-day slip, you cannot anticipate problems early enough to prevent them—you must wait until the problem is big enough to notice with the measures that you have. Then it will probably be too late to fix it, at least not without considerable pain.

THE ESSENCE OF RATIONAL MANAGEMENT

Figure 3.3 shows the four elements of rational management. Although I have already discussed each individual element, they are all related and are all required for an effective management style.

First, in setting product or operational goals, examine current performance and devise goals to meet business objectives. Then translate these long-term objectives into short-term goals that motivate action.

Second, require plans to meet the short-term goals. Goals drive plans and the people who will do the work must make

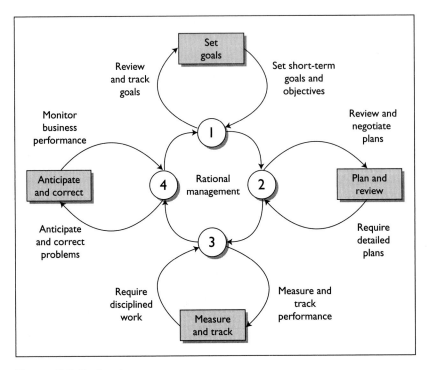

Figure 3.3 Rational management

these plans. Then have the engineers defend their plans and show you that they are complete and sufficiently detailed to guide the work. If a plan does not meet your goals, negotiate that plan to arrive at one that will meet your business needs and that the engineers will commit to meet. To work this way, the engineers must know how to make plans and they must be required to do so.

Third, measure and track the plans and monitor the discipline with which the work is done. Once you have a plan, you have a benchmark for measuring performance. To have any chance of meeting their commitments, however, the engineers must follow their plans, measure their work, and regularly report on their progress. This requires that they be trained in disciplined practices and that they measure and track their work and manage the quality of the products they produce. Then, of course, they must consistently follow these practices in doing the work.

Finally, continually monitor business performance. If you see problems, follow a rational management style to address those problems. When the work is planned, measured, and tracked, you can regularly monitor business performance. You will have a precise and timely picture of business status, and you can anticipate problems and take timely action to correct these problems before they impact business performance.

SUMMARY AND CONCLUSIONS

With a rational management style, you have precise data on the organization and can make sound and timely decisions. There are four elements to rational management:

1. Set aggressive long-term goals, but break these goals into realistic and measurable short-term goals.

2. Require detailed and complete plans, review these plans, and then negotiate the commitments with the people who will do the work.

3. Insist on facts and data, and use these facts and data to run the business.

4. Monitor the work, and use current data to anticipate and resolve future problems.

4
Why Quality Pays

As described in Chapter 1, quality must come first, even before the schedule. In the subsequent chapters, we have discussed some examples of poor software management. These stories all had an underlying quality theme. Testing was expensive and took a lot of time, the finished products were often highly defective, and the plans and data needed to be accurate and precise. These issues all concern quality.

Software quality is a growing problem and, based on current trends, these quality problems will only get worse—at least until executives start demanding quality software. There are three reasons to insist that software quality be measured and managed:

1. Poor-quality software can cause major property damage and even kill people.
2. Quality work saves time and money.
3. If *you* don't manage software quality, nobody else will.

POOR-QUALITY SOFTWARE CAN BE LIFE-THREATENING

As software becomes more widely used, the reports of problems are increasing. Although relatively few fatalities have occurred to date, many software defects have caused major disasters. Some examples are the following:

- Six people were killed when an incorrectly programmed medical instrument overexposed cancer patients to radiation.

- A manufacturing worker was killed when a software defect caused a production machine to crush him.

- A software error in the Ford Explorer engine controls limited vehicle speed to 110 mph instead of the specified 99 mph. At 110 mph, the Firestone tires on Ford Explorers had a rated life of ten minutes.

- At Bendix Brakes, a software design omission caused improperly installed brakes to release momentarily at speeds of less than 15 mph. No one was actually hurt, but the recall cost tens of millions of dollars.

- A software design mistake in the Mars orbiter caused this $125 million spacecraft to crash into the planet and be destroyed.

- Poorly designed software caused the pilot of a commercial airliner to mistakenly fly into a mountain, killing all the passengers and crew.

- A three-line programming error in an Intel manufacturing process caused a Pentium recall that cost the company over $400 million.

- The Code Red worm, by taking advantage of a common type of software defect, was able to infect 250,000 machines and cause widespread Internet shutdowns in just nine hours. The worldwide cost of preventing further Code Red infections was $1.2 billion.

QUALITY WORK SAVES TIME AND MONEY

In deciding how to manage software quality, we must first consider the facts. First, while developing programs, even experienced engineers inject a defect about every ten lines of code* (LOC) [1]. The programmers are not incompetent or lazy, they are just human. All humans make mistakes, but in software, these mistakes result in defects. This means that a modest-sized program of 100,000 LOC typically would start with about 10,000 defects.

The second key fact about software quality is that the cost of finding and fixing defects increases at every step in the development process. For example, Xerox has measured this time, and its data are shown in Figures 4.1 and 4.2 [2]. The defect find

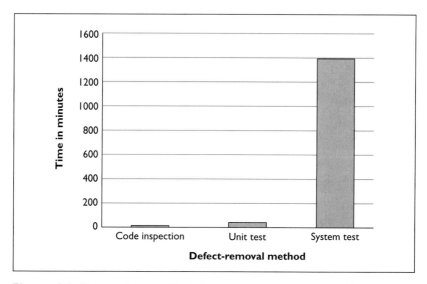

Figure 4.1 Time to find and fix defects

* The line-of-code (LOC) measure refers to the text lines in a printed program listing. One line is typically a short statement of 10 to 25 alpha-numeric characters. The KLOC measure refers to thousands of LOC.

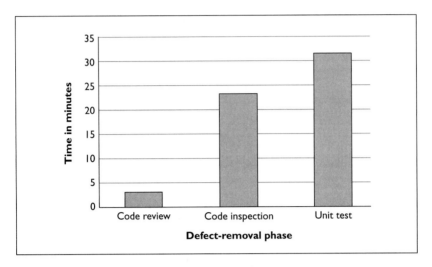

Figure 4.2 Time to find and fix defects

and fix times shown range from 3 minutes in code reviews to 25 minutes in inspections and 1,400 minutes in system testing. Engineers do code reviews by reading and analyzing their programs. In inspections, several engineers review a program to find its problems. In unit testing, each programmer tests the small program modules that he or she developed and fixes all of the defects found. In system testing, all of these small program modules are combined and tested as a complete system.

To appreciate the significance of these times, consider the time required to find and fix 10,000 defects. Using the Xerox data, the defect-removal time would be 4,170 hours with inspections, 5,330 hours for unit testing, and 234,000 hours for system test. Note that 234,000 hours is over 100 engineering years of work. Clearly, selecting the proper defect-removal method makes a big difference in both software development time and in engineering costs. As we shall see later in this chapter, defect-removal methods also have a big impact on the quality of the finished product.

The third key fact about software quality is that the engineer who developed the program is best able to find and fix its defects. This is demonstrated by the Xerox data shown in Figure 4.2. Here, in a review, an engineer personally reviews his or her program module to find and fix its defects. Instead of 25, 32, or 1,405 minutes per defect, the engineer who wrote the program module can generally find and fix its defects in just a few minutes each. SEI data show that the most efficient way to find and fix defects is for engineers to read and carefully analyze their programs. This takes them about an hour for every 100 lines of code. Engineers who do such careful reviews typically find and fix 5 to 10 defects per review hour. Therefore, counting review time, the average defect-removal time in code reviews is between 6 and 12 minutes per defect [1]. With code reviews, the engineers can find and fix 10,000 defects in only about 1,000 hours instead of about 4,000 hours with inspections, 5,000 hours with unit testing, or over 200,000 hours in system test.

Since reviews are so effective, you might wonder why everyone doesn't use them. The reason is that good code reviews require disciplined methods and special training. The engineers must gather defect data and use these data to help them find and fix the defects. Because people tend to make the same mistakes repetitively, these data show engineers what kinds of defects to look for. With few exceptions, engineers are not trained in such quality methods and do not believe that reviews and defect data would help them. Methods for convincing engineers to use such methods are discussed further in Chapter 6.

DEFECT-REMOVAL STRATEGIES

In the normal process of translating a program into testable form, about half of its defects are removed by a program called a compiler. Compilers are much like spell-checkers in that they identify most of the spelling, punctuation, and other syntax-type defects. That means that the compiler would find about half of the 10,000 defects in a typical 100,000 LOC program. To find the remaining 5,000 defects, the three strategies are to test; to inspect and test; and to review, inspect, and test. Since reviews and inspections typically do not find all of a program's defects, reviewed programs are inspected and inspected programs are tested to find even more of the defects.

Figure 4.3 shows the times and effectiveness of the three strategies for finding and fixing the defects in a 100,000 LOC software system. As you can see, the times required and the finished product defects are dramatically different. For example, the test strategy takes 23,400 hours, while the inspect/test strategy takes only 11,000 hours. Even less time is required by the review/inspect/test strategy, which takes about 6,000 hours, or only about one-quarter as long as the test strategy. The time savings come from finding more of the defects in reviews and inspections and fewer in system test.

Perhaps the most significant point about the test strategy is its ineffectiveness. Even after spending over ten engineer-years of work, the test strategy produces products with lots of defects.

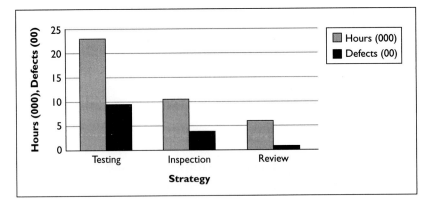

Figure 4.3 Defect-removal strategies

The inspection strategy takes half the time and leaves less than half as many defects, while the review strategy takes a quarter of the time and leaves one-eighth as many defects. Each of the defects remaining in a shipped product could damage your product's users and cost you hundreds of hours to find and fix.

The reason that testing takes so long is that a test reveals only the symptoms of a problem. Then the engineers must determine where the problem is in the system and its underlying cause. This is particularly difficult when there are multiple problems. Then the engineer must isolate the symptoms for the particular problem, identify the troublesome module, find the mistake, and then fix that mistake. After each defect is fixed, the fix must be installed in the system, and the system retested. Because each of these steps can take an engineer an hour to a week or more, the time to find and fix a few hundred defects can be many months.

QUALITY WORK IS MORE PREDICTABLE

Another benefit of quality work is a direct consequence of the unpredictability of testing. Since the time to find and fix each defect can vary from a few hours to several weeks, testing time will vary widely when products enter test with more than a very few defects. This means that any project with a large amount of testing work will be nearly impossible to plan and track. Therefore, if you want accurate plans and reliable commitments, you must insist on quality work.

IF YOU DON'T MANAGE SOFTWARE QUALITY, NOBODY ELSE WILL

An IBM example shows why executives must sponsor quality programs. In 1983, the president of IBM was concerned about the quality of IBM's software. While software quality was not yet a crisis, software maintenance costs had reached $250,000,000 a year. The president asked me to be IBM's director of software quality and process. My charter was to fix the software quality problem.

Some years earlier, management had issued a policy called Corporate Instruction 105, or CI-105. It required that the quality of every new product be better than the best previous IBM product of the same general type. The hardware groups had responded to CI-105 and made very substantial quality improvements. Most of these product managers had improved quality by ten or more times, and some had improved it as much as 1,000 times. However, the software community had not responded to CI-105. One division president even met with corporate management to argue that CI-105 could not be used for software. He said that software quality couldn't be measured, that software was inherently defective, and that they could not afford to do more testing. IBM's president and the other executives disagreed, and the division president was soon replaced.

To apply CI-105 to software we first needed a software quality measure. We established a technical task force to define this measure and assigned several members of my quality staff. We also included one or two engineers from each of the major software laboratories. After several months of work, this group had reviewed many possible measures. It was soon apparent, however, that the laboratory members were not authorized to agree to any measure. Since the experts from my group had learned enough from the task force to propose a usable quality measure, we decided to disband the task force.

After talking with several laboratory directors, I concluded that the software laboratories would not voluntarily agree with any CI-105 quality measure, so I had my staff draft our own proposal. We reviewed this proposal with corporate and division staffs and then sent it to the software laboratories. We told them either to agree with this measure or to propose a better one. While several laboratories reluctantly agreed, the largest and most important laboratory refused. The director disagreed with the idea of measuring software quality and would not accept *any* measure.

I scheduled a meeting for this director to explain to IBM's president why he did not want to measure software quality and what he proposed to do instead. When I told the director about this upcoming meeting, he became very upset. Rather than explain his position to IBM's president, however, he agreed with our proposal. We then quickly obtained agreement from the other laboratories.

At the time we established the CI-105 quality measure, we also defined how the measure would be used. The product manager was required to make a quality plan before a new or enhanced software product could be announced. After product shipment, my staff gathered defect data from the field engineering division every month, sorted these data by product, calculated the CI-105 measures, and posted the planned and actual data on an executive quality reporting system. Over the next several years, the measured quality of IBM's new software products improved by an average of 35% a year, or nearly ten times in five years.

I did not appreciate the significance of the CI-105 software-quality initiative until I later heard that marketing representatives at Amdahl Corporation, an IBM competitor, were reporting that IBM's software quality had improved dramatically. This was significant because Amdahl's customers used IBM programs to run their systems. When your competitors notice that your product quality is improving, you are making progress.

SUMMARY AND CONCLUSIONS

The following six principal points are made in this chapter:

1. Defective software is expensive and can even be life-threatening.

2. Software engineers inject defects because they are human.

3. The cost to find and fix a defect increases exponentially as development progresses.

4. The engineer who developed a program is best able to find and fix its defects.

5. Effective defect-removal methods require special training.

6. If you do not manage software quality, nobody else will.

REFERENCES

1. W. S. Humphrey, *A Discipline for Software Engineering.* Reading, MA: Addison-Wesley, 1995.

2. Allen Willett, a PSP instructor and TSP coach at Xerox, private communication.

5
Leadership Goals

G oals set the direction for the organization. If your goals are
short term, your people will think only about survival. But
if you want to improve the way your organization performs, you
must make improvement an important part of your organization's and managers' goals.

FASTER, BETTER, CHEAPER

In the early 1990s, the head of NASA was concerned about the
long schedules and high costs of NASA projects. He felt that the
work was overly complex and could be greatly simplified. To
change this situation, he initiated a new strategy called "Faster,
better, cheaper." Because NASA subsequently started launching
new spacecraft in a fraction of the time and for a fraction of the
cost of prior missions, the new strategy seemed to be a success.
Then along came the Mars orbiter and lander missions.

On September 23, 1999, the Mars Climate Observer, which
had been launched nine months earlier, crashed into Mars and
was destroyed [1]. NASA had another Mars mission on the way,
so they conducted three studies to find out precisely what had
gone wrong and to prevent the next mission from having the
same problems. The studies found several problems, with one
critical mistake in the software. Through a design oversight, two

separate parts of the orbiter used different measurement systems: one was metric and the other used inches and feet. This meant that the software controlling the mission actually gave incorrect commands and caused the orbiter to crash into Mars, destroying the $125,000,000 mission.

After considerable study, NASA felt that they understood what happened to the Mars Orbiter and that the Mars Polar Lander would not have the same problems. It didn't, but it had other problems. On December 7, 1999, the Mars Polar Lander also crashed into Mars and was destroyed. This time, the problem was a spurious signal that, when misread by the software, caused the lander's engines to shut off prematurely. It was another costly failure after a lot of expense and a long space mission.

While both the Mars missions had different problems, the problems had a common cause: system and software design and testing errors. In the rush to get the missions launched in minimum time and for least expense, the engineering teams had not paid sufficient attention to quality. After talking with management at NASA's Jet Propulsion Laboratory (JPL), which had developed and operated these missions, I concluded that the basic problem was in managing the "faster, better, cheaper" charge from the head of NASA. Although the objective was noble, the implementation was problematic.

A standard management principle is that what gets measured gets managed and what gets managed gets done. However, what does not get measured and managed often gets ignored. JPL knew very well how to measure faster and cheaper, but no one established measures for *better*. As a result, by measuring faster and cheaper and ignoring better, they actually got "faster, cheaper, worse." These multi-million-dollar missions were launched quickly, but they were total failures. So, without measuring all three parts of the goal, "faster and cheaper" turned out to be very expensive in the long run.

FIXING SOFTWARE IN AN ORGANIZATION

What executives find particularly frustrating about this story is that they know of no alternative to pushing for faster schedules, and anyone who ignores costs is destined for bankruptcy court. Also, the need for quality is so obvious that everybody should know about it, so why should anyone have to emphasize it? The problem is that most software projects are late, their costs are far over plan, and product quality is marginal at best. Although intolerable, this is the way most software groups have always worked. Unless you make changes, your organization will continue to work this way indefinitely. So it is clear that *you* must do something, but what changes should you make, and how?

There are three steps to fixing the software work in your organization. First, decide that you need to make changes. At this point in the book, you have probably already reached this conclusion. Second, decide what kind of software business you want. Without first defining the goal, there is little chance that you will get there. Third, with a defined goal, you can start making changes. This chapter deals with the goal. Subsequent chapters and the six book appendices describe how to make the required changes and what the changes will accomplish for your business.

ESTABLISHING THE GOAL

Just like NASA management, you probably want faster, better, and cheaper. To have any chance of actually getting better products on shorter schedules and for lower costs, however, you must be very precise about what you want. To start with, your basic objectives concern three principal topics: schedule, quality, and cost. You undoubtedly have other objectives such as people resources, technology leadership, or competitive superiority, but for now we will deal only with schedule, quality, and cost. Then you will see that when you do fully meet the schedule, quality, and cost goals, you will meet most of your other objectives as well.

In an engineering organization, if you want to change the schedule, quality, and cost of the work, you must change many parts of the business. And because the engineers actually do the work, your principal objective must be to impact what these engineers do. While you will hold the managers responsible for making the improvements, the real goal must be to change the way that the engineers work. A corollary is equally important: if the proposed changes do not change how the engineers work, then the changes will not significantly improve the schedule, quality, or cost performance of your organization.

While faster, better, and cheaper are nice overall goals, you cannot hold people responsible for them. Do you hold the engineers responsible for working faster, or is it a team job? How about the managers—what is their role? Similarly, to do better or cheaper work, everybody must be involved. Unfortunately, holding everyone responsible for meeting a goal has the same effect as holding no one responsible: no one owns the goal and nothing happens. Therefore, to actually get faster, better, and cheaper work, you need specific goals. Then, of course, you need to assign these goals and track them to ensure that they are met.

ACCELERATE THE WORK, NOT JUST THE SCHEDULE

The first thing to realize about the shorter-schedule goal is that it isn't what you really want. You want faster deliveries. The schedule is the plan or template for the job. Shortening the schedule without accelerating the work is a recipe for disaster. To actually speed up the work, you must focus on the tasks, how they are done, and what it takes to accelerate an engineering project.

To see how to accelerate a job, let's consider an example. How would you set the world record for building a house? The

San Diego Building Trades Council, in conjunction with many local builders and building trades, decided to do just that. They built a house in world-record time [2]. Starting with a dirt lot, two crews of 350 workers each raced to build, decorate, furnish, and landscape two nine-room houses in the fastest possible time. The winning team built and finished the house and had it passed by on-site building inspectors in just 2 hours and 53 minutes.

Since the normal time to build, inspect, and get such a house ready for sale was 90 days, it is easy to dismiss this as a trick. However, if you watch a video of the actual construction, you will appreciate what was involved. They added chemicals to heat the concrete so that it would set in 45 minutes; they had parallel teams for every possible task; and they had all of the materials on hand and ready. Nothing was prefabricated; they started with raw lumber, paint, and nails. However, they planned every step to the minute, and they built two complete practice houses the week before to test the process and to ensure that everybody knew precisely what to do. There was no waiting around, they just did their jobs. These were highly motivated teams. You could see the excitement and hear the cheering. The teams did an extraordinary job, and they loved every minute of it.

Although building a house and developing a software system are very different jobs, we can learn a great deal from the house-building example. Think about the challenge of getting 350 people to synchronize their work and to cooperatively do *any* complex task, let alone to do it in world-record time. First, to accelerate a job, the most obvious need is planning. Without a precise and detailed plan, 350 people could not possibly coordinate all of the tasks needed to build a house in 2 hours and 53 minutes. In fact, they probably could not have built the house in 90 days. These teams had detailed plans that showed what every worker would do for every minute of the job. The first requirement, then, is for detailed and comprehensive plans.

Second, the engineers—not the managers—must make the plans. Only the engineers know the job details, and only they can define all of the required steps. Third, the managers must ensure that the engineers are all trained to make detailed and accurate plans. Fourth, the immediate managers must participate with their teams in making the plans, and finally, more senior managers must review these plans for detail and completeness. If the engineers, teams, and managers meet all of these goals, you can be pretty confident that the work will be planned adequately.

After planning, the next requirement is to have the teams use their plans to do the work. In fact, one of the major benefits of having detailed plans is that teams can do workload balancing. This is what teams do when some members fall behind schedule and others are ahead. The early members can help the late members or rearrange the team's tasks. Workload balancing is an essential part of teamwork, and high-performing teams do it instinctively. In the house-building example, the same teams took about 6 hours to build two practice houses the week before. Because the workers learned how to better balance their work, these teams cut their building time for the same house from 6 hours to under 3. Think of that: with the same plans, workers, and materials, they built the identical houses in half the time! This is the power of workload balancing. It really accelerates the work. This leads to a key goal: to have the teams dynamically rebalance their workload, even every week if necessary.

Another obvious need from the house-building example is quality. There simply is not time to do the job over. In fact, of the two competing teams, the losing team was actually ahead until the inspectors found that the roof was placed incorrectly. The required adjustments were minor, but they took long enough for that team to lose the race. The quality requirement is discussed further in the next section of this chapter.

After quality, you need one more thing: motivation. It is clear from the house-building example that everybody on each team did their utmost to build the house in the shortest possible time. How do you get teams to work like this? Obviously, the engineers must be motivated, and the team must provide a motivating and supportive environment. Clearly, this is a crucial organizational goal: to have motivated engineering teams.

IMPROVING QUALITY

Next we consider quality goals. Saying that you want to improve quality is meaningless. Everyone wants to improve quality, but few people actually do it. A Teradyne team provides a good example of what is required. This team used the Team Software Process (TSP), which is described in Chapter 7 and the appendices of this book. Following the process guidelines, the engineers all measured and tracked their work, and managed the quality of their products. This team delivered a 90,000 LOC product six weeks ahead of schedule. The system had only two defects in customer acceptance testing and has had none since. By comparison with a prior much smaller product, this team reduced the defects the customer found in acceptance test by 250 times and cut the customer's testing time from nine months to five weeks. Needless to say, the customer was pleased.

The Teradyne engineers were all trained in quality methods, and they knew how to measure and manage quality. In every phase of the job, they recorded the time they spent, the defects they found, and the sizes of the products they produced. While the training took about ten days per engineer, Teradyne reported that the results with the first project paid for the company's entire investment in quality improvement [3]. This suggests a quality goal: that the engineers be trained in quality methods and that they use these methods on the job.

CUTTING COSTS

We have already discussed two of the most important cost-reduction steps: accelerating schedules and improving quality. Beyond these, the simplistic view is that you cut costs by improving productivity. Although this will often work for physical labor, it is a blind alley for engineering. Engineering is intellectual work and cannot easily be automated or accelerated. When managers tell engineers to improve productivity, the engineers hear "Hurry up." Unfortunately, this causes them to skip many quality-management steps like reviews, inspections, or unit testing. Since skipping these steps defers defect discovery and repair until system test, hurrying the engineers invariably extends testing time and ultimately increases costs and schedules.

Other than rushing the work, the principal thing you can do to reduce engineering costs is to help the engineers maximize the time spent actually working on the project. A detailed project plan consists of sequences of tasks that must be completed in the correct order and at the proper time to meet the project schedule. Task time is the time that engineers spend working on these scheduled tasks. Task time does not include time spent in meetings, on breaks, asking for management guidance, or on any of the other normal and necessary activities involved in engineering projects.

When they first hear about task time, most managers equate it with productive time and feel that all other time is somehow wasted. Therefore, managers think that the engineers' task time should be close to 40 hours a week. After a little discussion, they realize that the normal workday must include many nontask activities. Most people then conclude that 20 task hours a week would be reasonable. When engineers measure and monitor their task time, however, they typically find they have been working only about 10 to 15 task hours a week.

Figure 5.1 shows 15 months of average weekly task-time data from an Allied Signal team of about a dozen engineers.

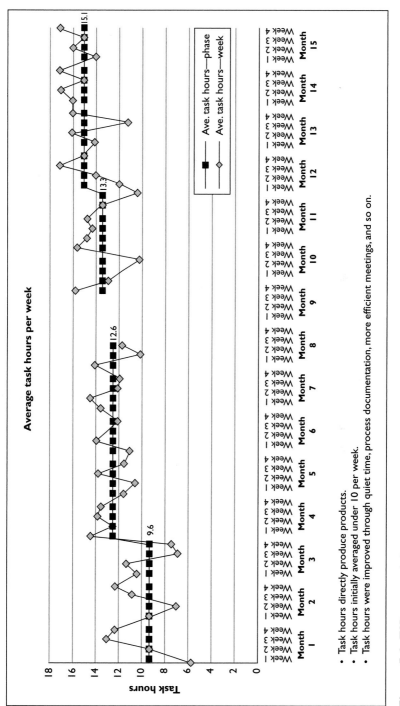

Figure 5.1 TSP team task hours

The first point at the left of the figure shows that the engineers averaged 6 task hours in the first measured week. Since the engineers were just starting to use the TSP, it took them a week or so to get used to the new methods. After that, their task time averaged about 10 hours a week. Moreover, by tracking their task time, the engineers saw how much time they spent on non-task activities. This motivated them to think of creative ways to be more efficient. It took a year for the Allied Signal engineers to improve average task time from 10 hours to 15 hours a week. Ultimately, with continued management support and encouragement, they reached 16 weekly task hours. By measuring and managing task time, this team achieved a 60% improvement in task time. Since it cost no more for engineers to work 16 task hours a week than 10, this was a substantial productivity improvement.

IMPROVING TASK TIME

Figure 5.2 shows the principal elements of task-time improvement. The four key aspects are task-time measures, engineer

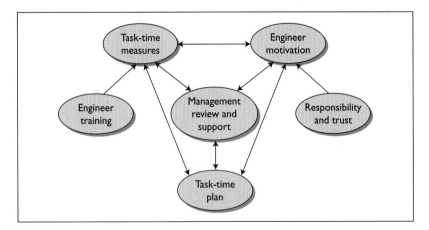

Figure 5.2 Task-time improvement

motivation, the task-time plan, and management review and support.

You cannot improve task time without task-time data, which can be gathered only by the engineers themselves. They must track their time in minutes and keep track of their interruption time. Engineers are surprised to find how often they are interrupted and how much time these interruptions take. One engineer told me that while she was working on a 108-minute task, interruptions took over 300 minutes. Because few engineers know how to measure task time—or even believe that these measures are useful—special training is required before they can measure and manage their task time.

If you ordered the engineers to increase their task time to 20 hours a week, they would lose any motivation to improve. Then they would likely report 20 hours and their actual task hours would probably fall. What is worse, you would never know what happened. To improve task time, you must motivate the engineers, trust them to set their own task-time goals, and help them with their improvement actions. Typical requests are for clerical support, morning quiet times with no meetings or interruptions, or working at home several days a week. With your help, the engineers can improve task time and their task-time reports will likely be accurate. Then you are likely to get a productivity improvement.

An interesting anecdote shows the impact that managers have on the engineers' task time. One week the Allied Signal management team held an off-site meeting with the customer's representatives. That week, the engineers' weekly task time jumped to well over 20 hours. On investigating, they found the reason for the sharp jump: management was not asking their normal questions, calling for information, or giving special assignments. All these actions cut into the engineers' task time and reduce engineering performance.

DEFINING RESPONSIBILITIES

It should now be clear that getting faster, better, and cheaper work involves many factors. At the most fundamental level, it requires a change in engineering behavior. The engineers must use disciplined methods, plan and track their work, and measure and manage product quality. The managers must initiate and maintain this new behavior, and you must establish the goals and track the work to put all these changes into place. The principal elements involved are shown in Figure 5.3.

To accomplish these objectives, the managers must manage the work, develop the workforce, and maintain an effective and attractive workplace. They must ensure that the engineers are trained in planning, know how to control quality, and regularly measure and manage their task time. The managers must also guide the teams' planning, monitor their plans, track task-time performance, and oversee product quality. Finally, the managers must help these disciplined and skilled engineers to build and maintain team motivation.

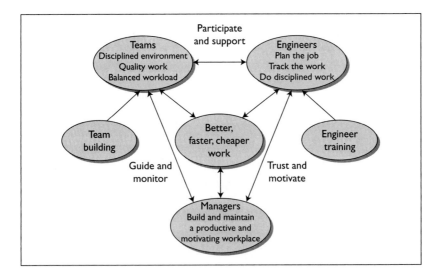

Figure 5.3 Setting goals

The team provides the working context for the engineers. It must provide a disciplined environment, ensure that everyone does quality work, dynamically balance the workload, monitor weekly task time, and track and report on project status. This calls for a team-building process and a management framework to guide and support the team's work.

Finally, it comes down to the individual engineers. They are the ones who actually develop the products. If you cannot change their behavior, not much else will change. The engineers must make detailed and accurate plans; record their time, size, and defect data; measure, manage, and report their task time; and be disciplined in using quality methods in all of their work.

This set of improvement goals is not as neat or simple as saying "faster, better, cheaper," but if your engineers, teams, and managers actually accomplish them, you will get faster, better, and cheaper work. It begins with changing engineering behavior, and ways to do this are discussed in the next chapters.

SUMMARY AND CONCLUSIONS

The following six principal points are made in this chapter:

1. In setting goals, make them clear and measurable, assign them to specific people, and track performance against them.

2. Goals that are measured get managed, and goals that are managed are often met.

3. Goals that are not measured and managed won't be met, and performance may actually deteriorate.

4. To improve engineering performance, you must change what people do.

5. To change their behavior, the engineers must know how to make detailed plans, manage quality, and use efficient working methods.

6. To actually improve the organization, the engineers must consistently use the methods they know and the managers must guide, support, and coach them in doing so.

REFERENCES

1. James Oberg, "Why the Mars Probe Went Off Course," *IEEE Spectrum,* (December 1999).

2. Four-Hour House Video. San Diego, CA: Building Industry Association, 1983.

3. Robert Musson. Presentation at the Software Engineering Symposium, Software Engineering Institute, September 1999.

6

Changing Engineering Behavior

C harlie ran a software group for a major bank and asked me
to join his staff meeting. Almost a year earlier, they had
started a process improvement effort, and he planned to review
their status. The corporate office had set a goal that every software group reach CMM* level 2 by the end of this year [1, 2].
After reviewing each department's status, we could see that this
organization had made little progress.

The process manager completed her report, and Charlie asked
for my comments. When I asked whom he held responsible for
reaching level 2, Charlie pointed to Beth, the process manager.
I told him that this was an impossible job; the only person who
can change a department's process is the department manager.
Beth could provide support and assistance, but there is no way
that she or any other staff person could change the way people
worked in any department but her own.

---

* The Capability Maturity Model (CMM) is a software process assessment
framework that guides management through a five-level improvement program.
At level 1, the organization's work is essentially unplanned and uncontrolled. At
level 2, standard planning, configuration management, and quality controls are
in place. At level 3, the organization has defined its basic processes and practices,
and at level 4, it has established and is gathering process measurements. Finally,
at level 5, the organization has a regular way to introduce technology improvements and to continually improve its processes. CMM and Capability Maturity
Model are registered with the U.S. Patent and Trademark Office.

vhether Charlie and his senior managers partic-
ank's bonus plan. Charlie said that they did.
f any of their bonuses depended on the process
work, he said that only his did. I then suggested
managers' bonuses to their process improvement
. Then Beth and her staff could assess the status of
nent each month and post the measures in Charlie's
room for their monthly management meeting.

and his managers agreed to make 25% of their
contingent on achieving their process improvement
l to track and review their progress every month. When
isited Charlie, six months later, all the departments had
d CMM level 2, and one was nearly at level 3. Once
s improvement was personally important to the line man-
, they made the needed changes very quickly.

IAT, NOT HOW

is clear from Charlie's experience, if you want to make changes,
e managers must agree and help to make them happen. If they
on't, not much will get done. So obtaining management agreement is necessary, but is it sufficient? Unfortunately, the answer
is no.

If your objective is "faster, better, cheaper," that requires
changing engineering behavior. Based on Charlie's experiences,
you might think that the managers could just tell their engineers
to change. This will not work. Software is an intellectual activity, and to direct software engineers to work in a particular way
is useless. Intellectual work cannot be ordered or directed. If the
engineers do not want to work as you direct, they won't, and
there's a good chance that you'll never know it.

Trying to change the behavior of software engineers is like
herding cats. They are very independent people; they all have

their own ideas, and they won't tell you what they think, particularly if they disagree with you. They just do what they want to do. Software engineers respond to guidance on what to do, but they resent being told how to do it. They properly see themselves as creative professionals. Over many years, they have developed a set of skills and capabilities, and they will not change these habits unless they are convinced that the changes will help them to do better work.

Most software engineers learn to write programs in high school or when they start college. Computer curricula typically concentrate on technical topics and do not address such subjects as estimating and planning, or how to measure and manage quality. Even when engineers have had planning courses, the subject is treated as something that managers do once at the beginning of the job.

Therefore, if you want your engineers to make detailed plans, to base these plans on historical performance data, and to adjust their plans as they do the work, you must provide them with the proper training. You must also convince them that planning, data gathering, and tracking are important and personally helpful. To gather data consistently, engineers must be expected to use the data. Of course, the managers must understand why detailed plans and disciplined work are important and how they will help their projects. So, to change the behavior of software engineers, you must convince both them and their managers that what you want them to do will help them and the business.

DISCIPLINED SOFTWARE PRACTICES

After 27 years with IBM, I joined the Software Engineering Institute (SEI). After a few years, the institute director named me an SEI fellow and gave me the opportunity to pursue my interest in quality management. The question I had long pondered was "If software engineers used the best known quality methods, could they consistently produce defect-free programs?"

My personal work as an engineer had been many years earlier, and subsequently I had learned a great deal about quality and quality management. Among other things, I had directed IBM's programming work, been IBM's director of software quality and process, participated in assessing semiconductor quality methods, and been on the Malcolm Baldrige Quality Award board of examiners. I had also led SEI's CMM development and helped many organizations use the CMM to improve their software capabilities. I had long believed that the typical software attitude of "build it quickly and fix it later" was wrong, so I decided to apply the quality principles I had learned to the task of writing programs.

When I started my research, I decided to call the method the Personal Software Process (PSP). My objective was to concentrate on how engineers personally write the small module-sized programs that form the building blocks for large programs. I believed that the quality of the product was determined by the quality of the process that produced the product. I further believed that a quality process must address all aspects of the work, including planning, tracking, and quality management.

The rationale for focusing on the quality of each engineer's personal work was that if every small program in a big system is not of high quality, the system cannot be of high quality either. Large programs generally have thousands of module-sized elements, and you can get a quality program only if every single module is of high quality. Therefore, the quality of every engineer's personal work is important. Improving average quality levels is not enough. For example, in a system with 1,000 modules, if 999 were defect-free but one was highly defective, the system would have a high average quality level. However, it would almost certainly have quality problems. Since every mistake by every single programmer contributes to quality problems, everyone on the project must do quality work.

I started my PSP research by defining a programming process and a set of measurements. Then I wrote the first program. In writing each program, I first made a plan, then I gathered data on the time spent by phase, I recorded every defect found, and I measured the sizes of the products produced. Over the next three years, I wrote 62 programs in several languages and I learned a great deal. I also found that, while PSP methods require considerable discipline, they produce high-quality programs. The PSP also improved my planning accuracy and my productivity.

CONVINCING OTHERS

Now that I had reams of personal data, I began speaking, writing papers, and meeting with engineering groups. I wanted others to use the PSP so they could see that it would work for them. I now knew that the standard quality principles used in other fields could be tailored specifically for software work and that, when they were, software professionals would produce high-quality programs in less time and on more predictable schedules than ever before.

People listened politely and one group of five engineers even agreed to try the PSP. They said they would use it when they had time. I called them almost every week; they never had the time. I concluded that when engineers work on real projects, they will not try anything new or unfamiliar. They are in a hurry and are unwilling to risk the learning time and unknown problems that invariably accompany new methods.

The engineers did not argue with my data, but they obviously did not believe that the PSP would help them. I needed to prove to each engineer that the PSP would help him or her do better work. Clearly, without data on their personal work, engineers would not try the PSP, but they could not get these data without using the PSP. While I knew that the PSP worked, I was stuck.

THE PSP COURSE

The answer to this conundrum was a course. Over the next year, I designed a PSP course, wrote a textbook, and taught the course at Carnegie Mellon University [3]. The results were better than I had hoped. Even more important, the student-engineers were convinced that the PSP worked for them. Several of them even changed their careers and are now working with me to transition the PSP into general practice.

The basic principles of the PSP course are shown in Figure 6.1. Since the purpose of the course is to convince engineers that the PSP will work for them, they must use it to write programs and gather data. To be truly convinced, however, they must write enough programs to learn the methods and gather enough data to show that their work has improved. This requires at least nine or ten exercise programs.

Before taking the PSP course, engineers must be capable programmers. Then they use the PSP to plan each program, use a defined process to write it, and gather precise data. They learn to plan, to use sound design practices, and to measure and manage quality. They also see from their own data that the disciplined PSP methods help them to do better work.

The PSP course results of 298 experienced engineers have been published by the SEI [4]. Examples are shown in Figures 6.2, 6.3, and 6.4. In these figures, point 1 at the left shows data for program 1 at the beginning of the course. Since the engineers have not yet learned the PSP, this first point represents their performance with their current software practices. Point 10

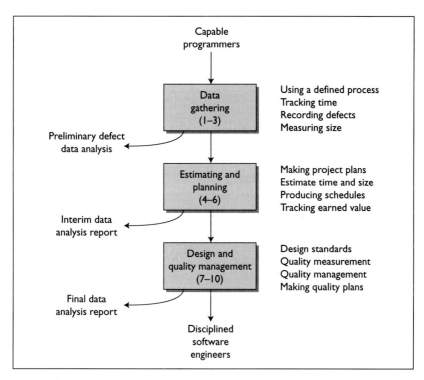

Figure 6.1 The PSP course

at the right shows their data when using the PSP. The difference is the improvement caused by the PSP.

Figure 6.2 shows how estimating accuracy improves. Point 1 at the left shows the estimating accuracy for program 1. Since the engineers have not yet learned estimating methods and have no historical data on their work, this first estimate is a guess. Point 10 at the right shows the estimating accuracy for program 10, the final course program. Here the engineers have learned how to use their historical data to make statistically sound estimates for program size and development time. They have also learned how to estimate the likely error range of these estimates.

As is clear from Figure 6.2, the engineers' estimating accuracy improves right up through the last program. This implies that

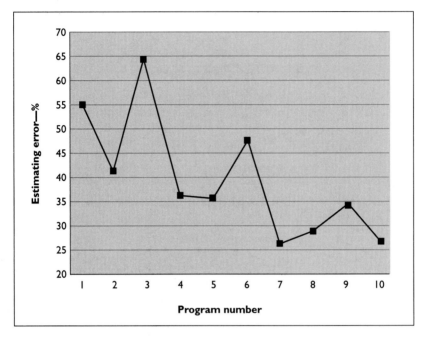

Figure 6.2 Time estimating error

estimating accuracy will improve even further, as long as the engineers continue using sound estimating methods and as long as they continue gathering and using personal data.

Figure 6.3 shows the defects these 298 engineers found in compiling and testing the ten PSP programs. Software engineers typically write programs quickly and then address quality during compiling and testing. With today's typical practices, engineers spend about half their development time compiling and testing. Even then, the resulting programs generally are defective. With the PSP, engineers concentrate on quality from the beginning, and they find and fix most of the defects before first compiling. They are surprised to see that by using the PSP, they reduce compile and test defects by five or more times and cut the time in compile and test by three or more times.

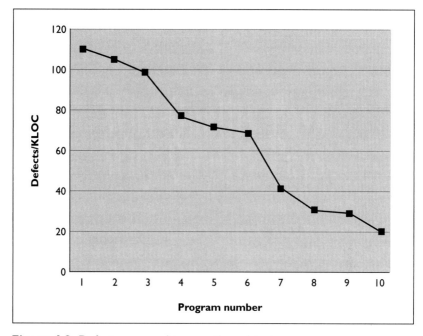

Figure 6.3 Defects removed in compile and test

For most engineers, the results in Figure 6.4 are most surprising. They see from their personal data that when they use the PSP to make plans and to track their time, size, and defect data, their productivity does not drop. In fact, for many, productivity actually increases. On average, engineers are as personally productive when they use disciplined methods as they are today. As we will see later, even when the engineers' personal productivity does not change, when they all make personal plans and measure and manage quality, their team's performance improves dramatically.

While over 90% of the engineers who take the PSP course are convinced of its value; a few are not. Most of them are like one young woman who told me, "I didn't believe the PSP would work, so I didn't use it." Rather illogically, she then claimed that

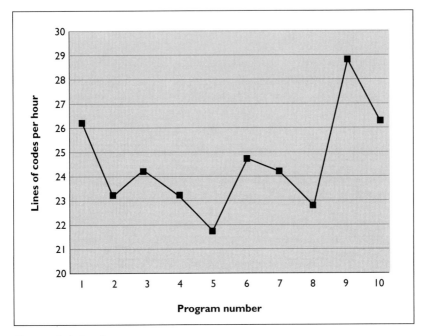

Figure 6.4 Productivity

her data showed that the PSP methods were not effective. Some engineers are so convinced their current methods are right that they will not try anything new. Some will ultimately see the benefits of disciplined methods, particularly if their peers use them, but a few will not. They tend to leave the organization when management insists that they use the PSP on the job.

COMING FULL CIRCLE

After the success of the PSP course, our SEI team started training engineers in industry and monitoring PSP performance on the job [5]. Although the initial results were positive, I was disappointed to find that PSP use died out shortly after course completion. Several engineers complained that they couldn't use the PSP because their managers objected to their making plans, gathering data, or doing quality reviews. As far as the managers were concerned, quality was for the testing department; the engineers should concentrate on coding and testing. We concluded that while PSP training was necessary, it was not sufficient. Engineers also needed a supportive working environment.

This should not have been a surprise. Disciplined performance in sports, the performing arts, medicine, or science all require the support of coaches, peers, and managers and the reinforcement of a professional working environment. The next step was to see if engineers would follow the PSP disciplines when they worked on teams where everyone was PSP trained and where management understood and supported the PSP practices. This leads to the next issue: how to build disciplined and motivated teams. That is the subject of the next chapter.

SUMMARY AND CONCLUSIONS

The following five principal points are made in this chapter:

1. For engineers to use disciplined methods, their managers must agree with the methods and support their use.

2. To actually change engineering and management behavior, the managers must be responsible for implementing the changes.

3. If software engineers are to change their behavior, they must believe that the new methods will work for them.

4. When engineers take the PSP course, they use disciplined engineering methods to write ten programs.

5. From their personal PSP data, the engineers see that by using disciplined methods, it takes them no longer to predictably write high-quality programs than it took them to write programs before.

REFERENCES

1. W. S. Humphrey. *Managing the Software Process*. Reading, MA: Addison-Wesley, 1989.

2. Mark C. Paulk, et al. *The Capability Maturity Model: Guidelines for Improving the Software Process*. Reading, MA: Addison-Wesley, 1995.

3. W. S. Humphrey. *A Discipline for Software Engineering*. Reading, MA: Addison-Wesley, 1995.

4. Will Hayes and James W. Over. "The Personal Software Process: An Empirical Study of the Impact of PSP on Individual Engineers." CMU/SEI-97-TR-001.

5. Pat Ferguson, Watts S. Humphrey, Soheil Khajenoori, Susan Macke, and Annette Matvya, "Introducing the Personal Software Process: Three Industry Case Studies." *IEEE Computer*, vol. 30, no. 5 (May 1997), pp 24–31.

7
Building Motivated Teams

My PSP experiences led to the development of the Team Software Process (TSP). The purpose of the TSP was to build an environment where everybody planned and tracked their work and measured and managed the quality of their products. The TSP was also needed to provide a management environment where the engineers are encouraged and rewarded for doing quality work. This would motivate them to use the PSP methods on the job. The experiences of the BrokerNet team of EBS show how effective this approach can be.

THE EBS BROKERNET TEAM

When we launched the BrokerNet team at EBS, Peter Bartko, the CEO, agreed to talk at the opening meeting. EBS operates an on-line worldwide currency-trading network for international banks. This system runs on EBS-owned computers and is controlled by EBS-developed software. On a typical day, it handles about $80 to $100 billion of currency trades. Since this system is updated frequently, EBS is continually modifying and enhancing the software. Before, the EBS engineers typically had spent many months testing each new product version.

In the fall of 1998, EBS management decided that they had to upgrade the entire system to a new technology called BrokerNet.

Peter Bartko, the CEO, decided to use the TSP to improve the quality of their software. Otherwise, he felt that the amount of testing required for a new system would be impractical. When he talked at the opening launch meeting, he described the company's business strategy and where this product fit in. He then discussed business opportunities and the date when the BrokerNet product was needed. He explained that the company was introducing the Team Software Process (TSP) because quality was critical and that the TSP process would help them to meet the company's quality goals. Although the delivery date was important, he said that the team's first priority was to follow the TSP process; speed was important, but if the team truly followed the TSP process and did high-quality work, they would end up with the fastest schedule.

At the end of the week, the team presented a plan with a much later date than Peter had wanted. The engineers explained that this was a large product and they did not see how to develop it any faster. Even though there were 47 engineers on the team, they needed 5 more to meet this date. While marketing was upset, Peter accepted the team's plan. He later told me that he would have liked the product earlier, but if this was the best the engineers could do, that was all he could ask. He didn't want this team to fail.

Most managers would say that Peter Bartko was crazy, that the only way to get software engineers to meet any kind of date is to push them. Peter was not being soft, however; he knew that he would get the best results if the team knew what he wanted and why. He trusted them to do their best. As our TSP results show, this is the most effective way to manage engineering teams. The way we learned this is the story of how we developed the TSP.

DEVELOPING THE TSP

By the summer of 1996, we had found that PSP-trained engineers could produce higher-quality products more predictably than ever before. However, we were dismayed to find that few engineers continued to use the PSP on the job after they were trained. Part of the problem was that no one else on their teams was trained and using the PSP. Another reason was that the organization's culture actually prevented them from doing quality work. All management ever asked about was the schedule, and quality was viewed as the testers' job. Since nobody else seemed to care about quality work and since their managers objected to their taking time to plan and review their work, few engineers were able to use the PSP after completing the training.

The obvious need was to build the proper kind of team-working environment. While I did not know exactly how to build a team process, I knew that I would never learn without building one. Therefore, my first step was to develop an initial version. Then I lined up two teams to use it. Unfortunately, these projects had to start in September 1996, when I had to be in Australia and New Zealand. Since I could not help the teams get started, I sent them a detailed process description.

After returning from the trip, I visited both teams. I found that the TSP had worked pretty much as planned. Both teams had made detailed plans and they were still tracking progress against these plans. However, I also found that these teams did not have the energy and motivation I had hoped for. The problem appeared to be in how we had started the projects.

HOW TO BUILD MOTIVATED TEAMS

Numerous studies have been made of team building and team motivation. The common thread is a teambuilding experience where the team works as a unit to accomplish some important and demanding task. The task we decided to use to build motivated software teams was the TSP team launch. The objective of the launch was both to excite the engineers about the job and to establish a mutual team and management commitment to the plan the team developed. To ensure that the launch worked properly, we defined a four-day launch process, used only PSP-trained team members, and had a trained and experienced TSP coach lead the team through that process.

The TSP launch starts with an opening meeting in which the entire team meets with marketing and senior management. These managers explain why the project is important and why the customers need the product. The team then makes a detailed project plan. At the end of the launch, the engineers present their plan to management, explaining how they plan to do the job and answering management's questions.

The best way to explain how this launch works is with the example of the first Teradyne team.

THE TERADYNE TEAM

When I launched the first TSP team at the Teradyne laboratory outside of Chicago, the general manager and the marketing manager attended the opening meeting. The general manager made some brief opening comments about the importance of the product and why it was needed in nine months. Then the marketing manager explained why the customers needed this product, and what the competitors offered. He concluded by stressing the importance of the nine-month schedule.

After the opening meeting, I met with the engineers and their team leader in a small conference room. This was an integrated team of hardware and software engineers. They were all in revolt. "Nine months! He's crazy! The last job took two years and it was a disaster. How can we meet this ridiculous date?"

After they had calmed down, I asked the engineers what management had said. They all answered, "We have to finish in nine months."

While I agreed that those were management's words, what did they mean? Again, the engineers said they had to finish in nine months. So I asked them, "Suppose you finished in seven months, would management take it then?" They all agreed that they would.

"So," I said, "management really meant that they wanted the job done as fast as possible, but that the fastest they thought you could do it was nine months, right?" They agreed. So I next asked them, "Do you always accept the first bid? How long do *you* think the job will take?" Next I asked them, "Whose date is the nine months?" They agreed it was management's. Then I asked, "Suppose you go to the general manager and say, 'Boss that's a terribly tight date, I don't see how we can make it,' but he insists and keeps on insisting on nine months. At the end of the meeting you say, 'OK, boss, if you insist, we'll give it our best shot.' Whose date is it now? It's yours, and don't you forget it!"

"So what do we do?" they asked. "You can't just guess," I replied. "Then management will prefer their guess to yours. Your best bet is to do your utmost to make a plan that meets management's objectives. When you have a plan you believe in, you will know if you can meet management's date or not. Then you can go back to management and convince them that it's a sound plan. You will have a date you believe in, and you will have a shot at making it."

The team got right to work. The engineers did a marvelous job. They followed the TSP process, laid out a system conceptual design, produced a development strategy, defined the process that they would use, and estimated the sizes of the system's parts. Next they defined the tasks for the entire job, estimated how long each task would take, and produced an overall plan and schedule. Their quality plan gave target defect levels for each phase and at delivery, and their detailed plans showed what every engineer would do every week for the next three months.

Finally, they analyzed the project risks and prepared a presentation for the final launch meeting with management.

When the engineers completed the plan, they were dismayed to find that the schedule was 18 months, not the 9 months that management had required. However, they knew it was an aggressive plan and the best they knew how to do. Going into the final launch meeting with management, the engineers were understandably nervous about management's reaction.

In the management meeting, the team leader explained what the team had done. When he got to the schedule, the general manager started asking questions. The team leader explained the size of the system and the amount of work they had to do. He compared this job with other projects and showed that the schedule was actually shorter than other similar jobs. The general manager was about to agree when the marketing manager exploded. "You'll destroy the business," he yelled. "The competitor has a better product on the market right now! We can't possibly hold the line for 18 months."

So I asked him, "You mean that the competitor is delivering a better product today?" He said yes. "Well, when do you think this competitor started developing this better product?" I continued. "It wasn't last week, was it?" Since he didn't know, I told him that the competitor probably started developing their better product a year or two ago. Then I asked, "Why didn't you start then? In the development business, if you can't anticipate the market, the engineers can't recover for you." The marketing manager subsided and the general manager accepted the team's date.

The following week, the marketing manager brought reinforcements to a meeting with the engineers. They spent a full day probing the schedule and trying to find any fat. The team answered every question by showing the work they had to do.

The engineers went through each of their tasks and reviewed the estimated sizes of all of the system components. They described how long it would take to specify and design each product element. In the end, the marketing manager said, "You really do have a lot of work to do, don't you?" He then accepted the 18-month schedule.

THE FINAL RESULT

These engineers did a remarkable job. They produced such a comprehensive and impressive design that, when marketing described it, the leading customers all waited for the new product. In the end, Teradyne didn't lose a single account. This team actually delivered the product six weeks ahead of the 18-month schedule, and the costs were below the plan. The product had higher quality than anything the company had previously delivered. It had only two defects in customer acceptance testing and none thereafter. Table 7.1 shows the team's original plan and what the engineers actually did.

I met with this team several times during the project and what most impressed me was the engineers' energy and enthusiasm. They were working hard, but they were having the time of their

Table 7.1 The Teradyne Team Results

	Plan	Actual
Size—KLOC	110	89.9
Effort—engineering hours	16,000	14,711
Schedule—weeks	77	71
Defects per KLOC		
Integration and system test	1.1	0.6
Field trial	0.0	0.02

lives. They were winners, and they obviously enjoyed it. This was a highly motivated team.

HOW DO YOU MOTIVATE TEAMS?

Motivated teams clearly do the best work—so how do you motivate them? In a business context, there are only three ways to motivate people: fear, greed, and commitment. While fear is an effective way to get action, it often engenders unthinking behavior. Fear-induced work tends to be unimaginative, slap-dash, and not very creative. The appeal to greed—paying big bonuses or commissions—works for some activities, but it has one big disadvantage: the need for precise measures. For example, sales quotas motivate increased sales volumes. However, depending on how quota performance is calculated, this may not produce higher profits. This is the "faster, better, cheaper" problem in another context. When performance is unmeasured or improperly measured, the results are often disappointing and can even be disastrous.

Unless your measures cover all important aspects, you will likely motivate counterproductive action [1]. For example, before the collapse of communism, the Soviet Union used five-year plans and production quotas to micromanage the economy. The Trans-Siberian Railway had goals for the number of cars crossing the continent. When the commissars found that the railway was sending empty cars, they required that the cars be loaded—the railroad filled the cars with water. Again, a simple measure motivated counterproductive behavior. For any but the simplest work, fear and greed are not effective motivators. That leaves you with commitment.

BUILDING COMMITTED TEAMS

To build a committed team, Teradyne first trained all the engineers in the PSP. This showed them how to plan their work and manage the quality of the product they produced. This action told the engineers that management was serious. Next, the general manager and marketing manager met personally with the team. This told the team that the job was important. Management also showed that they respected the engineers and wanted them to understand both the business and technical needs. In the process, they convinced the engineers that this was an exciting and important job that warranted their personal commitment.

Management also gave the team an aggressive date—so aggressive that the engineers didn't see how to meet it. Although overly aggressive goals can be demotivating, that need not be the case. Goals are demotivating when they appear unachievable as well as when they are too easy. To do their best, engineers need a challenge *and* they need a plan to meet that challenge. That is the key: an aggressive challenge is fine as long as the engineers can make a plan to meet it. But if the engineers feel that a schedule is impossible, they will either get discouraged or panic. When they panic, they throw all their good practices aside and start banging out code. Then they invariably take longer than they would have with a rational plan.

At Teradyne, instead of complaining about an impossible date or slapping out a poor-quality product, the engineers planned to do the job properly. They put in four grueling days and evenings to produce the best plan that they could. When the team leader presented the plan to management, all of the engineers were in the room and helped defend the plan. The managers asked many questions, but the engineers explained the plan and convinced them it was sound. This wasn't the team leader's plan; they all owned it, believed in it, and would do their utmost to meet it.

If you want committed teams, give them aggressive goals, but also have them make plans for meeting these goals. Ensure that every member is involved and that everyone knows how to make plans. Whether or not the plan meets your goals, have the engineers describe it and why they believe it is right. Show that you need this product and that the date is important, but also demonstrate your need for a meaningful commitment. Look for any fat in the plan, but also look for holes or omissions. You don't just want a promise; you want a realistic commitment that the team will meet.

If, as is often the case, the plan does not meet your needs, negotiate with the team. Add resources if needed, reduce product functions, or deliver in increments. Keep examining alternatives until you get a plan that the team will commit to and that you can accept. Then you will have a committed team.

THE EBS RESULTS

To protect themselves from teams that are habitually late, managers often set more aggressive dates than they really need. When you can count on your teams to meet their commitments, you get better results by being honest. At the EBS launch described at the beginning of this chapter, Peter Bartko, the CEO, told the engineers what he really needed. Even though their original date was not what he wanted, he was willing to wait to see what they could do.

After a couple of months, the EBS team completed the requirements and the preliminary design. The lead designer then saw how to deliver a simpler initial version of the product on Peter's originally requested date. The team agreed with the idea, so he talked with the marketing and technology people, who also agreed. The team then made a new plan to deliver this first product version the following August.

For the next ten months, the team followed this new plan and delivered the initial product version within three weeks of the committed date. While testing took about a month longer than expected, the product had higher quality than anything else they had ever developed. The BrokerNet system has now been installed and used in over a dozen international banks, with no reported problems.

A TRUSTING ENVIRONMENT

The EBS BrokerNet team voluntarily accelerated a schedule that management had already accepted. This is directly counter to the "give them an inch and they'll take a mile" view of traditional management. Many managers feel that if you don't demand an aggressive date, you will get a relaxed schedule that the engineers will still miss. I have never had a team give me a relaxed plan. In fact, teams generally make more aggressive plans than management would dare to make for them.

Engineers are smart people. They can quickly sense a lack of trust. When you don't trust them, they are not likely to trust you. Then they will never propose a more aggressive schedule than you have requested. Think of it this way: who truly understands the job and is in the best position to make an aggressive plan? Make sure that the engineers know what you need and, once they have done enough work to understand the job, they will often get better ideas. If you do trust them, they will keep thinking and, once they better understand the job, they are likely to devise creative ways to accelerate their work. They might even come up with a solution that no one could have imagined at the beginning. Peter Bartko demonstrated a great way to do this; he knew that the important question was when the product was *delivered,* not when it was *promised.*

THE CONSEQUENCES OF IMPOSSIBLE DATES

Since the Teradyne team had originally been given an "impossible" date and still did a great job, why not set an impossible date? With an aggressive date, the argument goes, the team just might meet it. I debated this question with the Teradyne team. I felt that, with PSP training and the TSP process, they could have resisted unreasonable management pressure even if I hadn't been there. They did not think so. Management had insisted on a 9-month schedule and they did not believe they would have had the nerve to present an 18-month plan. Experience shows however, that when properly coached, TSP teams create realistic plans and defend their plans to management. To date, of dozens of TSP teams, not one has caved in and committed to a date that the engineers did not believe in. Then, with few exceptions, these teams met their commitments.

If you push a team to meet an unrealistic schedule, you will likely get a disaster, regardless of the process your teams follow. Without strong support and a great deal of experience, teams rarely have the self-confidence to challenge their management. When the engineers start with a flaky plan, they don't have a prayer of meeting it. From a motivational perspective, this is the worst possible result: the engineers are working to your date rather than to a commitment of their own.

With an unrealistic date, teams take longer to produce poor-quality products that do not meet the user's needs. Then they spend more time fixing the product than it would have taken to do the job properly in the first place. Not only won't you have a motivated and committed team, you will be right back where you started: wondering how to get faster, better, and cheaper work from your software teams.

MAINTAINING TEAM COMMITMENT

Once managers have trained their engineers and followed the TSP process to launch their teams, they have just begun. Getting engineers excited about building advanced and sophisticated products is easy. However, the team generally will have many months of hard work and face dozens of unexpected challenges. Management's job is to keep the teams motivated and to ensure that they consistently do disciplined work.

In one organization, management supported an early TSP team through the launch process. Then the team began the job. Within a couple of weeks, however, management pulled one engineer off the job. Since he was needed permanently on the new job, they replaced him with another engineer who had not been PSP trained. This new engineer did not understand the plan or the process that the other engineers were following. Soon, management made another change and the team had another untrained engineer. Now the engineers started to argue about how to do the work. Soon, team discipline collapsed and the engineers reverted to their prior software methods. The project was a disaster.

Once you have trained and launched a TSP team, you must protect and nurture it. Add only PSP-trained engineers, and do not change membership unless absolutely necessary. Review team performance monthly or at least quarterly and have management follow project progress every week. Show continued interest in the work and regularly ask about quality. This book's appendices provide further guidance on how to launch and support TSP teams.

SUMMARY AND CONCLUSIONS

The following six principal points are made in this chapter:

1. To build a committed team, give its members aggressive goals and have them make a plan for meeting these goals.

2. Review the team's plan and have the engineers defend it.

3. If the team's plan does not meet your needs, negotiate with the team.

4. Once you have a plan that you can accept and that the team has agreed to meet, you will have a committed team.

5. With motivated and committed teams, projects will consistently deliver quality products on their committed schedules and for their planned costs.

6. The Team Software Process (TSP) shows you and your organization how to build and maintain committed teams.

REFERENCE

1. Robert D. Austin. *Measuring and Managing Performance in Organizations.* New York: Dorset House, 1996.

8

The Benefits of Teamwork

I t takes time and money to change any organization, and software groups are no exception. If you approach change in an orderly way, however, the benefits can be substantial. This chapter describes these benefits and summarizes the costs and the return you can expect. A return-on-investment analysis for a typical TSP introduction program shows that you will fully recover your costs within the first two years with an average five-year return of over 300%. Appendix F gives a more detailed description of this example.

By using the PSP and TSP, organizations have significantly improved the predictability and cycle time performance of their software groups. They have also reduced development costs, improved product quality, and reduced employee turnover. This chapter summarizes these benefits for five organizations that have introduced the TSP.

BETTER PREDICTABILITY

When I launched the TSP team at Hill Air Force Base* in February 1998, Hill management had already signed a contract

---

* Hill Air Force Base is the first U.S. government organization to reach CMM level 5. This is the highest level of performance CMM defines for software organizations, and only a few dozen groups in the world have reached it.

to deliver the team's product in September. Also, the team had just learned that its air force customer had scheduled a training exercise for August and the program manager wanted the product a month earlier. He needed to demonstrate the new product in this training exercise.

When the Hill team completed its plan, the engineers found that they could finish the project in August as the customer had requested, so they committed to that date. After working on the job for a couple of months, the engineers were significantly ahead of even this accelerated schedule, so they asked the project manager what he wanted them to do. They could either finish early and give back some money, or they could add more functions to the product and finish on time. The customer opted for adding the functions, and the team delivered on schedule [1].

This is normal for TSP teams. When engineers are properly trained and use disciplined methods to plan, track, and manage their work, they consistently deliver quality products on schedule. What is more, they know precisely where they stand and can predict when they will finish. From an SEI study of 28 projects in four organizations, the quartile range of schedule performance is shown in Figure 8.1 [2]. Of these 28 projects, 13 used the TSP and 15 did not.

The black portion in Figures 8.1 to 8.5 shows the performance range for the middle 50% of the population, the top and bottom limits of the population are shown by the top and bottom horizontal lines, and unusual or "outlier points" are shown by the circles and asterisks.

SHORTER CYCLE TIME

The first TSP project at Boeing was to make a major modification to a large military avionics system. In the launch, manage-

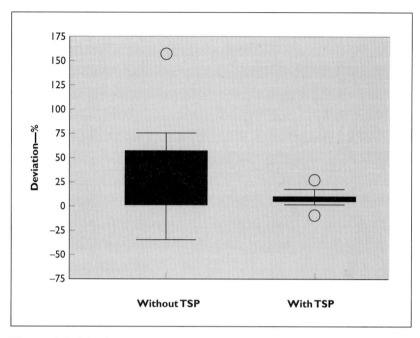

Figure 8.1 Schedule error

ment told the team that the product had to be delivered on schedule and that any delay would disrupt the flight testing program. This would be very expensive. Since this was the first time the company had used the TSP, management did not realize that disciplined teams produce more complete and higher-quality designs than other software groups. Therefore, the managers were concerned when the engineers did not complete the design on the date of the previously committed design milestone. Because the product had much higher quality than they expected, however, testing time was sharply cut and the overall schedule was shorter.

Because of their personal attention to quality, these Boeing engineers reduced test defects by 75%. Compared with previous projects, this cut test time by 94%, and the product was delivered

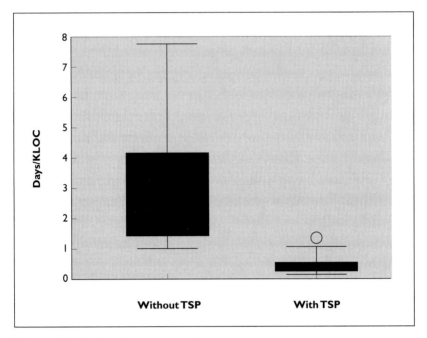

Figure 8.2 Reduced system test time

ahead of schedule [3]. This is typical of disciplined teamwork. As shown in Figure 8.2, the SEI study of TSP projects found that system test time is reduced by about ten times [2]. Because, as we saw in Chapter 6, the time required to write high-quality programs is no more than the time to produce defective ones, quality work sharply cuts development cycle time.

REDUCED DEVELOPMENT COSTS

Teradyne had gathered final system testing and field maintenance defect data for ten years. They found that their previous products had averaged 20 defects per 1,000 lines of code (KLOC). Therefore, a typical 100 KLOC product would have 2,000 defects in system testing, field testing, customer acceptance testing, and customer use. Since it cost an average of 12 engineering hours to find and fix each such defect, the defect repair costs for typical products were several engineering years of work.

When Teradyne introduced the TSP, this normal 20 defects / KLOC defect level was reduced to 1. This saved the company $5.3 million in the first two years [4]. From the SEI study of 28 projects, Figure 8.3 shows the quartile range of improvement for test defects, and Figure 8.4 shows the quartile range of error in planned versus actual project costs [2]. With the TSP, fewer defects mean lower costs and more accurate cost estimates.

IMPROVED PRODUCT QUALITY

As described in Chapter 7, EBS operates an on-line worldwide currency-trading network for international banks. This system runs on EBS-owned computers and is controlled by EBS-developed software. EBS develops and tests new feature upgrades in

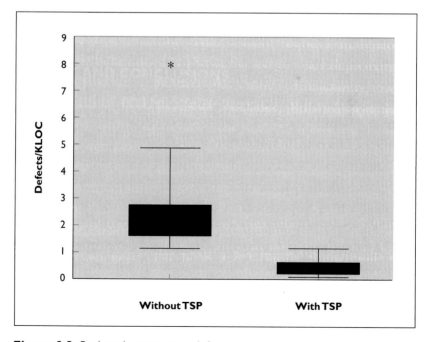

Figure 8.3 Reduced system test defects

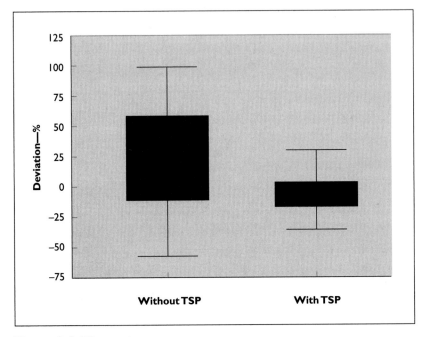

Figure 8.4 Effort estimate error

their laboratory in New Jersey. Then these upgrades are handed to an internal test group that runs another entire suite of tests. Finally, when everything seems to work properly, they turn the product over to a quality assurance group for final acceptance testing and quality certification. This involves another exhaustive batch of tests. Because of the time previously required to find and fix the many defects normally found in this process, test and certification often took longer than the rest of the development phases combined.

While the development team spent a year developing the first BrokerNet version, final testing only took 13 weeks. Perhaps most interesting is the fact that, when properly trained and led, TSP teams improve as they gain experience with the process. Version two of BrokerNet was nearly twice as large as version one, and it completed system testing in only eight weeks. It also

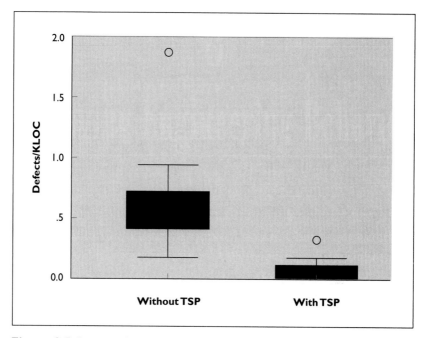

Figure 8.5 Improved product quality

had only one-third as many system test defects. Version one of this system has now been installed in over a dozen customer offices in Europe and has worked flawlessly without a single reported problem. This kind of quality performance is typical of TSP teams. As indicated by acceptance test defect densities in Figure 8.5, the defects in completed TSP systems generally are at or very near zero [2].

REDUCED EMPLOYEE TURNOVER

When I launched the first TSP team at Kaiser Electronics, the team plan showed that they needed five additional PSP-trained engineers in four months. Since this group was located in San Jose, California, and programmers were then in very short supply, I felt they would have trouble hiring that many engineers so quickly. The department manager told me it would not be a problem. The word was out that they were using the TSP and several engineers had already called looking for jobs.

When I returned a year later, I asked the Kaiser president about their experience with turnover. He explained that annual turnover in Silicon Valley was typically around 25%. The prior year, Kaiser turnover had been 23%. In software, their turnover was 7%, but on the TSP team it was zero. This again is typical of TSP teams. Once the engineers see that their initial concerns about planning and data gathering are unfounded, they like the personal control that the TSP provides them. They also feel proud when they deliver quality products on time. As many engineers have told me, now developing software is fun. In a tight labor market, the principal constraint on growth is the ability to hire and retain good people. A reputation as a good place to work is money in the bank.

TSP INTRODUCTION COSTS

Regardless of how attractive some new method or technique appears, it usually comes with hidden costs and problems, so most executives are reluctant to make major investments without an initial prototype trial. This is a wise approach.

TSP introduction costs vary considerably, depending on the strategy you select. For example, for maximum speed, you would need the most outside assistance. Conversely, if you wanted to minimize external support costs, you could train your own experts and have them handle the training and introduction work. A modest initial TSP introduction program would involve management and engineer training for two or three teams of engineers. This would be followed by a TSP launch for each team.

The costs to retain outside experts to provide the initial training and to lead the managers and a couple of engineering teams through these steps could vary considerably. In the organizations I have worked with, these costs typically have run between $100,000 and $300,000. Depending on the project schedule, you would then have initial team results in 6 to 12 months. At that point, you could make an informed decision on a broader introduction program.

RETURN ON INVESTMENT

Improving the performance of an organization is an investment, and to make a rational decision on this investment, you would need a return-on-investment analysis. One way to judge the affordability of making such an investment is in terms of avoidable costs. Because using the TSP cuts testing time by about ten times and ships essentially defect-free products, a good place to start is by examining the costs of poor quality. The two categories of avoidable quality costs that are easiest to measure and estimate are final testing time and customer-reported defects. Assuming you had a 100-engineer software organization that used current common software methods, your annual avoidable quality costs would be $6.5 million. For more detail on these calculations, see Appendix F.

By introducing the TSP, organizations have typically reduced test time by 10 or more times and defects by up to 250 times. The example in Appendix F assumes that you would cut test time by a conservative 4 times and customer-shipped defects by 10 times. As shown in Figure 8.6, the likely TSP savings would then be $3,750,000 for testing and $1,350,000 for defect repair costs, or a $5,100,000 annual savings from the improved quality your teams produced by using the TSP.

To determine the benefits of the TSP for your organization, you need data on costs before the change and an estimate of these costs afterward. Because software work typically is not

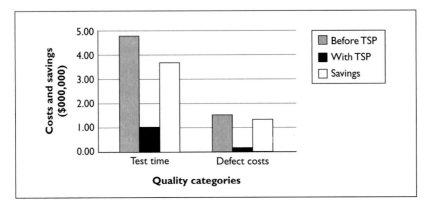

Figure 8.6 Quality costs and savings

measured or tracked, however, few organizations can get the "before" data required for such an analysis. The next paragraphs summarize a typical example return-on-investment analysis. For a complete description of this ROI example, see Appendix F.

The example in Appendix F covers all of the costs and savings for introducing the TSP in a 100-engineer organization. The total costs are $1,728,000, and the annual savings, once TSP is in full use, are $5,100,000. The total introduction costs therefore are returned in only four months of full TSP use, with an ROI of 291%. If your organization has more than 100 engineers, the costs and savings would be proportionately larger. You could also reduce the introduction costs by training your own PSP instructors and TSP coaches, then use them to train and coach your teams. This would take longer and delay the TSP savings, but it would be less expensive.

DISCOUNTED RETURN ON INVESTMENT

The quarterly cost and savings profile for a TSP introduction program are shown in Figure 8.7. At a 6% annual interest rate, the present-value cost of a five-year TSP introduction program

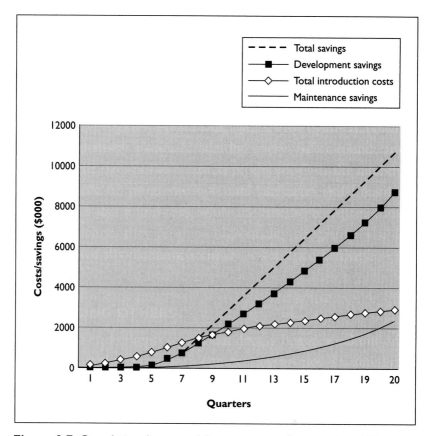

Figure 8.7 Cumulative discounted 5-year costs and savings from TSP introduction—6%

is $2,805,810, and the present-value savings is $11,151,963, for an ROI of 397%. At a 10% annual interest rate, the five-year present-value costs would be $2,524,350, and the savings would be $9,277,230, for an ROI of 368%.

It takes about two years for the cumulative TSP savings to surpass the cumulative introduction costs. This time is required for training and for the first TSP projects to reach the testing phase. The post-release defect savings build more slowly because of the time required for TSP-produced products to reach the users. Since the TSP savings are not realized until the latter phases of the projects, it takes about two years to fully recover the TSP introduction costs.

SUMMARY AND CONCLUSIONS

The following seven principal points are made in this chapter:

1. The benefits of introducing the TSP are better predictability, shorter cycle time, reduced development costs, improved product quality, and reduced employee turnover.

2. An initial TSP introduction program should train and launch two or three trial teams.

3. In parallel with these initial teams, organizations should train their own PSP instructors and TSP coaches.

4. After the initial projects are launched successfully and the organization has its own qualified PSP instructors and TSP coaches, it should expand the TSP to other groups.

5. Total TSP introduction costs are returned in about four months of full TSP use, and the ROI is 291%.

6. At a 6% annual interest rate, the five-year present value ROI is 397%.

7. The cumulative investment recovery period for TSP introduction is about two years.

REFERENCES

1. David Webb and Watts Humphrey. "Using the TSP on the Task View Project." *Crosstalk: The Journal of Defense Software Engineering* 12, 2 (February 1999).

2. Donald R. McAndrews. "The Team Software Process (TSP): An Overview and Preliminary Results of Using Disciplined Practices."

Carnegie Mellon University Technical Report CMU/SEI-2000-TR-015, November 2000.

3. John Vu. "Process Improvement in the Boeing Company." *Proceedings of the 2000 Software Engineering Process Group (SEPG) Conference.* Seattle, WA: March 2000.

4. Robert Musson. Presentation at the Software Engineering Symposium, Software Engineering Institute, September 1999.

9
Next Steps

You are the only person who can transform your organization's culture. Although many people must be involved, you must set the direction and motivate the managers and engineers. Then, once the required changes are initiated, you must ensure that these changes are maintained and that your people use the new methods in their work. This chapter reviews the seven steps required to implement the methods described in this book.

THE SEVEN TRANSFORMATION STEPS

If you take these seven steps, you will change the culture and improve the performance of your software operations. If you skip even one step, the transformation process will be delayed and may not even be successful.

Step One: Establish a Quality Policy

Tell your people that quality work is your first priority. Write and issue a policy saying that the right way to do a job is always the best way. Emphasize that doing poor-quality work to meet a tight schedule is not acceptable; when people do this, they are breaking company policy and you want to know about it. When such cases are brought to you, insist that the policy be followed.

There will be many objections, but don't waver. This policy will effect a fundamental change in the organization's culture and is the essential first step toward getting consistently high-quality work from your software people. With software, quality work always pays.

Step Two: Identify an Improvement Champion

Because every engineering organization must give priority to its technical work, process improvement cannot be the engineers' or managers' top concern. You need a champion to ensure that the line managers do not neglect this important responsibility. This champion will conduct status reviews and identify problems. The champion's job is to maintain management's focus on the TSP transformation, and the champion must have process improvement experience as well as the skills to advise and assist engineering groups.

The champion should start by establishing a plan and a schedule for installing the TSP. The plan should be reviewed with the product managers and adjusted until both the champion and the managers agree. Then you should review this plan to ensure that it is both practical and aggressive. The change effort will almost certainly face resistance and require support. If you do not regularly monitor and support it, the TSP improvement effort will not survive.

Step Three: Set Precise and Measurable Goals

To achieve difficult objectives, people must have clear goals and measurable benchmarks. To change your organization, define precisely what you want to achieve and convince everyone that this goal is important. Then, to sustain the improvement effort, measure and regularly track progress against it.

Feedback is an essential part of any challenging human activity. Think of a basketball game where the score is tied and there are three minutes to play. The place is alive. People are on their feet. The enthusiasm and energy are infectious. But suppose no one knew the score; instead of an energized team, the players would be tired and wondering how soon they could quit. There would be no energy, no enthusiasm, and probably no game.

Give the line managers specific goals to build and maintain their TSP teams. Insist that they properly train and professionally launch these teams. Assign these goals to all senior managers and ask for specific percentages of teams to be using the TSP at the end of each calendar year. Have each senior manager give you the date when the first TSP team will be launched and further dates for when 25%, 50%, 75%, and all the teams will be following the TSP. Then track these goals and make sure that the managers are serious about meeting them.

All TSP teams should have the goal of faithfully following the TSP process. This means they must do quality work, regularly report on their projects, and maintain a disciplined engineering environment. Further, all team members should track their size, time, and defect data and use these data to track project progress and manage product quality. Each team should quantify its goals during its first launch and review these goals with management at each relaunch and project review.

Every engineer should also have a personal goal of following the disciplined PSP practices. This calls for detailed personal plans; tracking time, size, and defect data; and consistently using quality methods. The team leaders should quantify these goals, negotiate them with each engineer, and track them every week. Performance against these goals should be part of the performance review and salary increase program.

Step Four: Hold Line Managers Responsible

This step is particularly important in large and bureaucratic organizations. Bureaucracies know how to resist change. They have learned to look attentive, appear active, and produce responsive results without actually changing behavior.

For example, even though your organization can pass some CMM or ISO process review and get the desired level 3 or ISO rating, the people may not be working any differently. In their zeal to meet management's aggressive improvement goals, process groups often establish all of the required documentation but do not disturb the engineering work. Although process people cannot change engineering behavior quickly, they can change documents and procedures quickly. Unfortunately, changing procedures without changing behavior will not improve business performance.

To improve the performance of your organization, you must improve the way that the people work. The only ones who can do this are the workers and their immediate managers. If you hold the line managers responsible for delivering products and make a staff person responsible for introducing and maintaining the TSP, the line managers will ignore the TSP and concentrate on the projects. The engineers will then continue to work pretty much as they always have. To make the transformation happen, the line managers must be responsible for TSP introduction and use in their own departments. The process and quality people then can support the teams and monitor and report on their performance.

Step Five: Provide Improvement Resources

Engineering organizations are difficult to improve for three reasons. First, improvement takes work. Someone must teach courses, coach teams, draft policies, document procedures, and develop and review standards. Someone must also get the engineers to take the courses, follow the practices, and comply with the standards. If you don't provide resources for doing this work, it will not get done. Second, the engineers are busy with development work and will not voluntarily attend courses, participate in planning, or be PSP instructors or TSP coaches. Third, few engineers know how to make the needed changes on their own, so they need experienced leadership and help. Someone must lead the working groups, set up and chair the review and approval meetings, teach courses, launch and coach teams, and monitor the engineering work.

The best way to set up an improvement activity is to establish what is called an SEPG (software engineering process group) and put the champion in charge. Then make the TSP program this group's first priority. The SEPG need not be large, and much of the work can be done by engineering task groups, but these groups must be led by specialists from the SEPG.

Step Six: Establish Priorities

When I met the commanding officer of the air force's Standard System Center in Montgomery, Alabama, the organization had been reviewed and assessed by many different groups. The most recent review group had submitted a report with 53 recommendations. The colonel's staff had reviewed these recommendations and found that it would cost $13,000,000 to implement them all. Because the report offered no guidance on which recommendations were most important, he did not know where to start. His organization ended up doing nothing.

Since there is always room for improvement, process improvement should be a never-ending process. If you try to do everything at once, however, you will accomplish nothing. The key to process improvement is to identify a few areas for improvement and concentrate on those. Once these areas are under control, move on to the next. If you continue improving and don't let the program die, you will ultimately transform your organization.

For TSP improvement, identify two or three projects to start with and get them working properly before starting any more. As the managers acquire more experience and as you build the resources to teach, launch, and coach TSP teams, you can accelerate the improvement pace.

Step Seven: Provide Continuing Oversight

This is the most important of the seven steps. If you do not personally believe that the TSP transformation is important, it cannot work. But if you believe that the TSP is important, hold your top managers personally responsible, regularly review status, and do not accept excuses, you will get rapid results.

You should also expect some resistance. There is never a convenient time to make a change, and there is always some crisis that "must" delay training. Although you should consider each case, if you too readily agree, you will get lots of excuses. Remember that if you don't insist on making changes, your people will continue to work as they always have. Then your organization will not improve.

THE ACTION PLAN

While these seven steps will transform your organization, you will also need a plan to guide the work and to help you track progress. It is surprising how often executives launch a well-conceived improvement program but fail to establish responsibilities or make a follow-up plan. If you do not define specific responsibilities and follow-up dates, all of the improvement planning will be wasted and nothing much will happen.

The first step is to get a detailed plan with defined actions, named responsibilities, and follow-up reviews. A typical set of actions for a TSP improvement program is as follows:

1. Issue the quality policy yourself, and do so right away.

2. Have the laboratory manager assign a champion to guide and direct the transformation program. This person should be named and on board in 30 days.

3. Within 60 days, the location general manager (with the champion's assistance) should arrange for the senior managers and executives to attend the TSP executive seminar.

4. Within 90 days, the champion should develop a plan for PSP training and launching the first two TSP teams. This plan should schedule team and manager training and identify two instructor/coaches. Use this plan as a basis for setting measurable goals for the managers.

5. Within 90 days, the program managers (with the champion's assistance) should identify the initial two TSP teams, their team leaders, and team membership.

6. Within 120 days, the managers of the two initial TSP teams should attend TSP management training.

7. Within 120 days, the champion should develop a long-range plan to introduce the TSP across the organization. Use this plan to update the managers' goals.

8. Within 1 year, every program manager should have PSP trained and launched at least one TSP team.

9. Within 2 or 3 years, depending on organization size, every team should be using the TSP.

This is a hypothetical plan, but it indicates the actions and responsibilities needed to introduce the TSP. When you conclude each review, identify the actions needed before the next review and who will take them. While the champion can make plans and schedule courses, the line managers must be held responsible for every action that involves their people. When the improvement champion is responsible for engineer training, for example, the managers will often pull them from the courses for a last-minute crisis.

While you should plan to personally hold the first few of these reviews, you may later wish to delegate this responsibility. Then require a written report of each review. Have your staff check the report to ensure that the actions have all been addressed, that new actions are specified, and that they are all assigned and tracked. To demonstrate your continued interest, contact the managers who conducted the reviews and ask some questions. Remember, you launched the program, and if you do not show continued interest, it will soon die.

SUMMARY AND CONCLUSIONS

People often argue that organizational transformation is difficult, but it is not. What is difficult is maintaining a management focus on the work. To ensure that your organization is actually changed, follow these seven steps:

1. Establish a quality policy.
2. Identify an improvement champion.
3. Set precise and measurable goals, with a tracking system and frequent reviews.
4. Hold line managers responsible for transforming the groups they manage.
5. Provide improvement resources, such as establishing and staffing a process group (SEPG).
6. Establish priorities.
7. Provide continuing oversight and show continuing personal interest in the transformation program.

In taking these steps, require a specific action plan with named responsibilities for each action and a follow-up date.

Software is an important part of your business, and it will be more important in the future. If your software people do not consistently meet their commitments with quality products, your business will suffer, and it could even fail. To run your business and to maintain a competitive position in your market-place, you must have a superior software capability.

This book outlines a strategy for a software transformation that has worked for other organizations and will almost certainly work for yours. By taking the seven steps described in this chapter, you will have a superior software capability, and you will have it sooner than you thought was possible.

A

The TSP Process

As described in Chapter 7, the Team Software Process (TSP) was developed to address the growing need for capable software teams that deliver quality products on schedule and for their committed costs. This appendix provides a brief overview of the TSP process. For more information about the TSP process, consult the other appendices and the available references [1, 2]. The topics covered in this appendix are

TSP overview

Team preparation

Inadequate preparation

TSP OVERVIEW

The TSP process was designed to build and maintain motivated and committed engineering teams. There are five requirements for motivated teams:

1. The team members are all skilled and capable of doing the job.

2. The team has an aggressive and important goal that the members must cooperatively accomplish.

3. The team members believe that the goal is achievable, and they each have a defined role in achieving that goal.

4. The team members have a common process and plan that guides them in doing the work and in tracking their progress.

5. The team leader supports and protects the team and keeps the members informed of management issues and team progress.

These five requirements must all be present for teams to be consistently motivated and to be fully effective in doing their work.

To build and maintain such teams, the TSP has the elements shown in Figure A.1. First, team preparation is required so that all members have the requisite planning, measurement, and tracking skills. Training is also needed so that the engineers can use defined processes, know why and how to measure and manage quality, and understand how to consistently make and meet commitments.

During the team launch, the team sets its goals, assigns team-member roles, and develops a team plan. The team members also develop detailed personal plans for their own work. After completing the launch, the team does the work, and management periodically reviews its status. The team leader holds weekly status meetings to provide the members with precise and timely feedback on their performance. The periodic management reviews help to maintain the engineers' motivation and commitment to the job.

After TSP teams have worked for several months, they will need a TSP relaunch. The relaunch process is much like the launch process and includes goals, roles, and detailed replan-

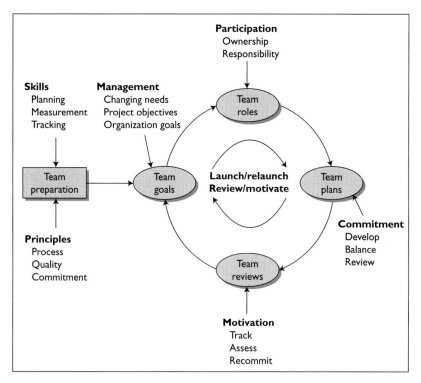

Figure A.1 The TSP process

ning. It is needed because detailed plans can cover only a few months of work. After that, the team members will need a relaunch to update their personal plans and to adjust for any other project changes in requirements, team membership, or the engineers' knowledge of the job. A periodic relaunch will keep the team's plan useful, current, and accurate.

Managers often worry that the engineers will slip the project schedule when they make a new plan. This is a question of trust. The engineers are committed to the current plan and will not change it unless they must. You can properly ask them to defend the changes, and if they truly need more time, the earlier you know it the better.

TEAM PREPARATION

The principal launch preparation activities are selecting the team leader, assigning team members, training the team members, and training the team leader and other involved managers. Teams also find it helpful to do some advance work on the project development strategy and product conceptual design. While these items will be produced during the launch, their quality impacts the quality of the plan, so advance preparation is usually helpful. An SEI-authorized TSP coach should work with your people to ensure that all of the required launch preparation work is completed on time.

TSP TRAINING

The TSP process produces motivated and committed engineering teams, but it will not work without proper training and management support. For example, Figure A.2 shows a family of six TSP courses that are required for the team members, their managers, and involved senior managers and executives. The six course topics are shown in the columns, and the participants for each course are shown by the horizontal arrows.

The bottom arrows in the left-most column show that senior managers and executives attend only a one-and-a-half-day seminar on TSP concepts. This is called the TSP Executive Strategy Seminar.

The second arrows from the bottom show the training for the other managers and team leaders. After covering the executive-level topics, these managers complete lectures and exercises on people and team management. All told, their training takes about three days.

The team members do not normally attend the executive or manager courses. They must be trained in defining and using processes, making process and product measurements, planning

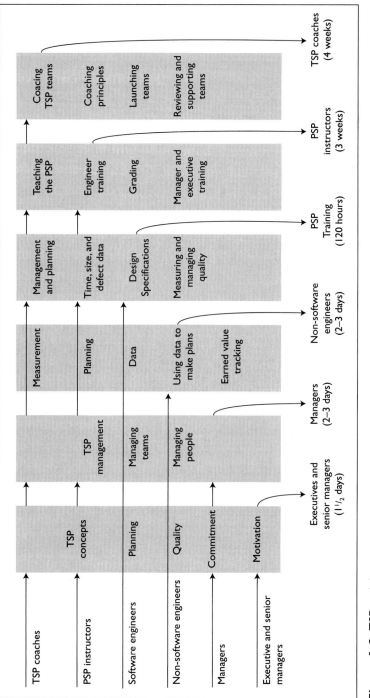

Figure A.2 TSP training

and tracking the work, and measuring and managing quality. This software engineer training is provided with the Personal Software Process (PSP) course, as described in Chapter 6 [2]. For software professionals, PSP training takes about 120 working hours and usually is done in two one-week training sessions that are spaced a few weeks apart. Several days of homework are also required.

Team members who are not developing software, such as requirements people, testers, and writers, must also be trained in measurement and planning. Then they can participate in the team launch, team management, and team operation. This training takes about two days. While it would be desirable to train all team members on quality measurement and management, that course material requires writing nine or ten module-sized programs, so only competent programmers can complete it.

The top two arrows in Figure A.2 show the training required for PSP instructors and TSP coaches. Since TSP teams require ongoing coaching and support, organizations should train and qualify some of their own people as TSP coaches and PSP instructors. These people would then be able to teach the four left-most courses in Figure A.2, and launch and coach the TSP teams.

INADEQUATE TEAM PREPARATION

Without strong executive direction and support, managers generally are reluctant to interrupt their projects for two weeks to get their software people PSP trained. In one example of the need for executive leadership, we conducted the one-and-a-half-day TSP Executive Strategy Seminar for 17 program managers. These managers each had several hundred people in their groups and were responsible for a number of large projects. While they all agreed that their projects were in trouble and that the TSP was what they needed, they also argued that management would not agree to their delaying the work long enough to train their people. Every project was critical, and they could not even foresee a time when training would be possible.

Early the next morning, I met with the vice president and general manager of the location and explained that these managers were acting like victims. Unless given clear direction, they would continue to wallow in their current problems indefinitely. The general manager agreed to meet with the program managers immediately and tell them they were to make plans to adopt the TSP and to tell him what it would cost and how it would affect their projects. When we next met with the program managers, everyone was able to make a training plan with relatively little project impact.

Proper training is essential. Without it, the engineers cannot follow the TSP process, they will not know how to plan and track their work, and they will not be able to measure and manage the quality of their products. Even worse, they will not believe that these actions are necessary or even desirable. When team members are not properly trained, the TSP process will not work.

In another example, management planned to train the engineers but encountered a last-minute crisis. When the coach arrived for the launch, he was told to proceed anyway; management said they would train the engineers later. Because they had not been PSP trained, however, the engineers did not know how to produce a plan or even understand why they needed one. After a few hours, the launch coach gave up trying to convince them to make a detailed plan. The team never did get trained or launched, and the company wasted all its management training and introduction effort. Most important, software engineering performance remained unsatisfactory. Inadequate training wastes time and money. Before participating in a TSP launch, everyone must be properly trained.

SUMMARY

The following five principal points are made in this appendix:

1. The TSP process is designed to build and maintain motivated and committed teams that consistently do quality work.

2. For a TSP team to be successful, the team leader and all team members must be selected and trained in advance.

3. For the launch to be successful, it must be led by a qualified TSP launch coach.

4. This coach will work with management and the team to ensure that the proper preparation work is done.

5. Without proper training, the TSP process will not work.

REFERENCES

1. Watts S. Humphrey, "The Team Software Process," *SEI Technical Report*, CMU/SEI-2000-TR-023, November 2000.

2. W. S. Humphrey. *A Discipline for Software Engineering*. Reading, MA: Addison-Wesley, 1995.

B

Launching a TSP Project

The TSP team launch is the most important single step in building a motivated and committed team. To be successful, the senior executive who initiated the team's project must attend the opening and closing launch meetings. These meetings will take only an hour or two each, and your presence is needed to build the team's commitment and to ensure that the team plans to do the job the way you want it done.

This appendix briefly describes the TSP team launch process. After an overview of this process, it describes the opening launch meeting and why you should attend it. Appendix C then describes the closing launch meeting and why your participation is also important. For more information about the TSP process, consult the other appendices and the available reference [1]. The topics covered in this appendix are

The TSP team launch

The opening management meeting

Team questions

Example opening meetings

Answering questions during the launch

The final management meeting

THE TSP LAUNCH

As shown in Figure B.1, the TSP team launch process includes ten meetings over a four-day period. The launch is a challenging and important task that requires that all team members work together to produce a comprehensive plan. They must participate in making the estimates, and they must agree on the final result. When a group is challenged with an important task and the members work together under skilled guidance, they generally form the personal relationships needed for effective teamwork. When engineers successfully complete a TSP launch, you generally have a cohesive team.

The launch product is a detailed plan. The team members must be trained for and guided through this launch. When they finish, they will know the tasks they must complete, as well as precisely how and when to complete them. They will also know how to produce a team plan quickly.

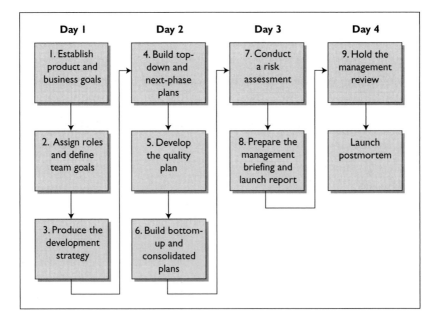

Figure B.1 The TSP launch process

In launch meeting 1, you describe why the project is important and what you are counting on the team to do. In meeting 2, the team defines its goals and selects team-member roles. These roles build team-member ownership and provide a degree of engineering control over the working environment. In meetings 3, 4, 5, and 6, the team builds its task, schedule, and quality plans.

Once the engineers have produced their plan, they conduct a risk assessment in meeting 7. Here they consider all of the principal project risks, rank them by likelihood and impact, and assign the highest-priority risks to team members to track. The team also devises mitigation actions for these high-priority risks.

Finally, in launch meetings 8 and 9, the team prepares a management presentation of the plan and reviews it with you. In effect, it is responding to your request in meeting 1. This is a traditional commitment process in which one party makes a request and the second responds with a bid and a plan to meet that request. Assuming that you and the team agree on the plan, then all parties will be committed to it. Once the engineers have made this commitment to you, they are motivated to meet it, both by their obligation to you and by their commitment to each other.

During the launch, the engineers define their own process and development strategy and agree on a plan to do the work. They also produce detailed personal plans and define their interdependencies with each other. These steps usually will build a motivated and committed team that feels in control of its work. Of course, this assumes that you support the team and agree to its plan.

THE OPENING MANAGEMENT MEETING

If you are the senior executive in the opening launch meeting, you should make a few initial remarks. Most engineers have participated on projects that started with great fanfare and then were killed after the engineers had done several months of hard work. Engineers don't like to waste their time; they would like some assurance that this project is real and won't be killed the minute somebody upstairs gets another bright idea. Just telling them that the project is important and won't be killed is pointless, because they already know you believe that—management has felt that way about every project, or they wouldn't have started it. One way to convince them of the job's importance is to explain how it supports the organization's long- and short-term goals. One engineering executive did this by describing the corporate strategy, the business objectives for the next five years, and how this project would contribute to those objectives. What most interested me was how often the engineers referred to these corporate objectives while producing their project strategy and plan.

After discussing the business objectives, explain why you have come to this launch and why you want to introduce the TSP. The TSP process has helped many organizations to improve, but it will not work unless the engineers faithfully follow it. The best way to convince them that the process is important is to make the process the first priority and the schedule the second priority. Emphasize that the *right* way to do the job always turns out to be the fastest and best way. Then tell the engineers that you are counting on them to do the job the right way.

If you tell the team that the schedule comes first and then mention that process compliance is important, the engineers will almost certainly shortchange the process when they feel pressed to meet the schedule. Since projects invariably end up in a schedule crunch, this will likely result in quality problems, excessive testing, increased costs, and a longer schedule. If you emphasize the importance of the process, you will get a quality product faster than would otherwise be possible.

If this is the first time your organization has used the TSP, also explain that you expect this team to set an example for how the TSP can improve the organization's performance. Explain that the TSP is an important step in the organization's improvement program, and that you are counting on them to demonstrate how well it works.

Next, realistically discuss the business goals for the project. Many managers give their teams artificially tight schedules. Aggressive schedules can be motivating, but they are motivating only if the engineers believe that they are real and can be met. An artificially tight schedule is a mistake for three reasons. First, the team will do its best to produce an aggressive schedule, regardless of the date you set. I have never seen a TSP team pad its estimate. Second, if you set an arbitrarily early date, the engineers will not know what you really need. They are then less likely to produce an optimum plan. Third, if the plan the engineers present does not meet your artificial date, they will quickly sense from your reactions whether or not the goal was real.

The best approach is to be honest with the team. If the project has a contractually committed milestone, for example, tell the team about it and why it is important. If one particular objective is critical but others are flexible, explain that as well. Explain the situation so that the engineers will understand the true business needs when they develop the plan. In concluding your comments, emphasize the importance of quality. In engineering, quality workmanship pays. Higher quality means fewer defects, fewer defects mean reduced testing, and reduced testing means accelerated schedules. So, by developing a high-quality product, the team will get the lowest costs and the shortest possible schedule.

TEAM QUESTIONS

Although it would not be appropriate to discuss the team's plan in the opening meeting, the team members need to understand what you want them to do. The meeting agenda contains a period for discussion, but the engineers rarely ask any questions. This is unfortunate, because they can produce an optimum plan only when they understand what you want.

If the team members start asking questions, there is no problem; but this is unlikely. The team leader or launch coach is more likely to ask the questions. Answer in a way that encourages more questions. If the team is to develop a product to address a competitive threat, for example, ask if any of the engineers knows about the competitive product and what makes it attractive to customers. You might ask about maintainability, service costs, security, or any other area that concerns you. Before concluding the opening meeting, make sure that the engineers understand what you want them to do. After all, if they don't know what you want, you are not likely to get it.

EXAMPLE OPENING MEETINGS

Although TSP teams generally have been successful once launched, the opening management meetings do not always inform and motivate the engineers. Typical problems are illustrated by the following examples.

The Missing Executive

In one case, no senior manager showed up for the opening meeting. The team leader explained management's views, but it was clear that management was not interested in the project. Not surprisingly, the job was canceled in a couple of months. The team leader did her best, and the engineers valiantly completed the launch, but they were doing it for themselves. Nobody else was interested.

If you or other senior managers attend only the highest-priority launches, the engineers will soon know which projects are worth their efforts and which are not. If a project is exploratory, explain what is needed to make it a success. If you are not sure that the project should be finished, settle that question before starting the launch. If there are questions you cannot answer without some engineering work, explain that and ask for the engineers' help addressing the open issues. If the project is important, attend the opening and closing launch meetings. If it is not important, don't start it until it is worthy of your and the engineers' time.

The Underemphasized Need

The company president attended the opening meeting and described the product and when it was needed. He then mentioned that he also needed programming support for a customer demonstration in early August. Since that was all he said about the demonstration, the engineers did not understand its importance. In making the plan, they found that the work to support this demonstration would seriously disrupt their development strategy, so they did not include it in the plan. Because of this miscommunication, the engineers did not give sufficient priority to the demonstration and it was ultimately delayed, causing a serious marketing problem.

When something is really critical, make sure that the engineers know it and why. Provide them with a list of your key needs and highlight those that are most important. If the engineers don't understand what is most important to you, they are likely to ignore your real priorities and work on what they *think* you said was important.

The Busy CEO

The company CEO said she strongly supported the TSP and that she would personally attend the opening launch meeting.

She also instructed the key engineering managers to be there. The CEO and all of the senior managers showed up for the first meeting, and the CEO made a few opening comments. She then explained that she had an important engagement and would have to leave. Shortly after that, the other executives also left. Soon, the only people left in the meeting were the team, the team leader, and the launch coach. Needless to say, this was not an effective way to launch a project. If you go to the opening launch meeting, stay until the end; but if you can't go, send somebody who will stay for the entire meeting.

ANSWERING QUESTIONS DURING THE LAUNCH

During the TSP launch, teams often find that they cannot meet management's desired schedule. The TSP process suggests that they discuss this issue with management as soon as they have done enough work to understand it. They do this to warn you of the problem and to give you an opportunity to think of how to address it. Assuming that the team leader or launch coach alerts you to such a situation, you could help the team by suggesting one or more acceptable alternate approaches. Before offering these suggestions, you might find it helpful to read the material in Appendix C.

THE FINAL MANAGEMENT MEETING

When the engineers have completed the plan, they will present it in the final management meeting. Attend that meeting, both to show your interest in the project and to ensure that the plan is properly reviewed and approved. Your role in the meeting is to probe the team's plan and to satisfy yourself that it was properly made, is suitably aggressive, and is realistic. This is what the engineers will be doing for the next several months or years. Since it presumably is important that they meet their commitments, this final meeting is to ensure that their plan will allow them to do so. The final management meeting is discussed in Appendix C.

SUMMARY

The following six principal points are made in this appendix:

1. The TSP launch is the most important single step in building motivated and committed teams.

2. To make TSP teams successful, you or some other executive or senior manager must attend the opening and closing launch meetings.

3. If you cannot attend these meetings or do not have time to stay for the full meeting, send an executive who can.

4. In the opening meeting, you should explain the reasons for introducing the TSP and the benefits the business expects.

5. If this is the first time the organization has used the TSP, stress its importance and how this project will help the company's improvement efforts.

6. In commenting on the project requirements, be candid with the team. To make an optimum plan, the engineers must understand the real needs for the project. Only then can they make the trade-offs needed to produce a superior plan and product.

REFERENCES

1. Watts S. Humphrey, "The Team Software Process," *SEI Technical Report*, CMU/SEI-2000-TR-023, November 2000.

C
Reviewing a Project Plan

This appendix describes the final TSP launch meeting and your role in that meeting. It covers the subjects to review and the questions to ask. It also includes a brief Plan Assessment Checklist to guide you in this review.

THE EXECUTIVE ROLE IN TEAM BUILDING

When engineers complete the TSP launch process, they present their plan in a final management meeting. You or some other executive or senior manager must attend this meeting. When no senior manager shows up for the final meeting, the engineers feel that they have wasted their time and their work is not important. One key reason for holding the launch is to motivate the team and get them excited about the job. Your participation will help do this.

During the final launch meeting, ask questions. This will help you to understand the engineers' plan and will demonstrate your interest in the work. The principal mistake that many senior executives make is to not ask enough questions. Not only does this imply that you are not interested in the team's plan, but it also misses an opportunity to ensure that the engineers have a plan they can meet and that this plan will produce the product you want on a date you can accept.

The team has spent several days producing a detailed plan to do the job that you asked them to do, and the team leader has just presented it to you in the final management meeting. Suppose the plan includes a later date than you had asked for. What should you do? The answer is discussed in more detail in the following paragraphs, but the short answer is to probe the plan to identify any mistakes or omissions. You may find that the engineers have allowed more time for some activities than is reasonable, but this has never been my experience. I almost always find that the engineers have overlooked things that, when included, will actually lengthen the schedule.

After you have satisfied yourself that the engineers have produced a credible plan, you still may not be happy with their date. However, now you know that this is the best available estimate for the job. If the team produced a schedule that was longer than you requested, they also should have produced several alternative plans to show what they could do with more resources or how the product could be delivered in versions. You can explore these alternatives with the team to see which make the most business sense. You can also try to think of other options that would better fit your needs.

If the engineers' plan or one of their alternatives is acceptable, the team will have a sound basis for doing the job. If not, they may be able to estimate some other alternatives on the spot, or they may have to come back in a day or so with a revised plan. At the end of the meeting or possibly a day or so later, you will have a plan on which you and the engineers agree. You will also have a motivated and committed team. Another important result is that the team will have a detailed process and plan for doing the work.

THE FINAL MANAGEMENT MEETING

In presenting the team's plan, the team leader will follow the LAU9 script shown in Table C.1. This is an example of the scripts that TSP teams follow in producing their plans and in doing their work. The TSP process uses scripts to guide engineers in consistently doing a job. A script is like the checklist that pilots use before a flight. It does not tell them anything they did not already know, but by following it they are less likely to forget things or to make mistakes.

In following the LAU9 script, the team leader first asks two team members to fill the time-keeper and recorder roles. These roles are specified by the TSP to help teams hold efficient meetings and to record and track important decisions. Once these roles are selected, the team leader will review the meeting agenda and objectives, describe the work done during the launch, and compare the team's plan with your goals. He or she will also discuss any alternate plans and review the risks that the team sees in meeting the plan.

After the team leader's review of this work, there is time for discussion and questions at step 7 of the LAU9 script. You could ask questions at any time during the meeting, but the team has done a great deal of work and will present a lot of information; by waiting until the discussion period, your questions will be better informed and less likely to cover topics that the team will later address.

THE LAUNCH PRODUCTS

In presenting the team's plan, the team leader will show the results of the team's planning work and distribute copies of many of the launch work products. The typical products of a team launch are shown in Figure C.1.

Table C.1 TSP Launch Meeting 9—Script LAU9

Purpose	To guide the team through the final launch management meeting
Entry Criteria	• All participants are present (launch coach, team members, team leader, management and marketing representatives). • For distributed teams, remote members participate via videoconference. • The management briefing guidelines were reviewed before the meeting. • Copies of the launch products and team presentation are available. • Forms: ITL, MTG, PIP

General	• In the management meeting, the team reviews with management their project plan and any questions or issues on the plan.
	• If management asks the team to modify or provide an alternate plan, the team needs to understand
	  – the desired plan changes
	  – what resource or work content changes to plan
	• Under no conditions should the team agree to a new schedule or plan without taking time to study and replan the work.
	• Meeting 9 generally takes 1 to 2 hours, depending on team size, project status, product complexity, and the team's TSP experience.

Step	Activities	Description
1	Meeting Roles	Select the meeting roles (specification ROLE). • The launch coach leads the meeting (script MTG). • The timekeeper tracks time and keeps the meeting on schedule. • The recorder notes meeting decisions and actions and writes the meeting report (form MTG).
2	Agenda and Objectives	The team leader reviews the meeting agenda and objectives.
3	Overview of Work Done	The team leader or a team member hands out copies of the launch products, reviews the launch process, and describes how the plan was produced.

136

Step	Activities	Description
4	Team Goal and Plan Comparison	The team leader or a team member summarizes the project goals. • management's stated and implied goals • a summary of the team's plan and goals • how the team's plan and goals compares with management's goals
5	Alternate Team Plan	If an alternate plan was prepared, the team leader or a team member distributes and reviews the alternate plan and the expected impact.
6	Risks	The team leader or a team member reviews each key project risk. • summarizes the risk's likelihood and schedule impact • discusses mitigation recommendations for high-impact risks
7	Discussion	The team leader asks for any questions and closes the meeting.
8	Launch Meeting Documentation	The recorder completes form MTG. • lists the attendees and the time spent by agenda item • describes decisions made and by whom • documents pending actions: what, when, and by whom • verifies the meeting report with the meeting attendees and gives the completed form MTG to the planning manager

Exit Criteria	• Management agrees with the team plan or resolution actions identified and responsibilities assigned. • All issues have been recorded (form ITL). • All process improvement suggestions have been recorded (form PIP). • The meeting report has been completed (form MTG and attachments). • The planning manger has copies of all meeting products.

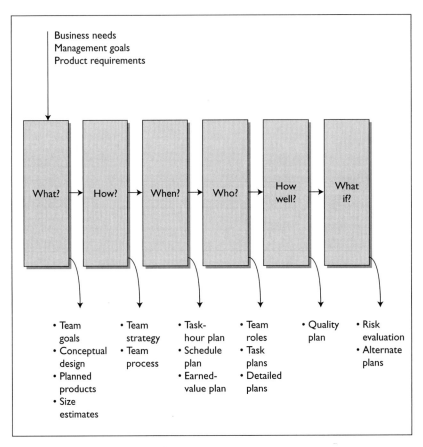

Business needs
Management goals
Product requirements

What? → How? → When? → Who? → How well? → What if?

- Team goals
- Conceptual design
- Planned products
- Size estimates

- Team strategy
- Team process

- Task-hour plan
- Schedule plan
- Earned-value plan

- Team roles
- Task plans
- Detailed plans

- Quality plan

- Risk evaluation
- Alternate plans

Figure C.1 TSP launch products

These products describe the team's plan in considerable detail. In addition to helping the team agree on what to do and how to do it, these launch products also provide the detailed guidance needed to do the job. Since these products are produced principally to help the team do the job, you need not review or attempt to understand them. They are distributed both to demonstrate that the team has done a complete job and to provide backup material for answering your questions. The launch products are briefly described in Table C.2.

Table C.2 Launch Products

Product	Description
Team goals	In addition to your goals, the team should have quality goals.
Conceptual design	The conceptual design • identifies the product elements • describes the engineers' current concept of the product they plan to build
Planned products	The team lists all the products to be produced.
Size estimates	The team estimates the sizes of all the principal products as well as the major elements in the conceptual design.
Team strategy	The team's development strategy covers such issues as multiple versions, prototyping, and integration plans.
Team process	The team process is built on the organization's process.
Task-hour plan	• The task-hour plan shows the planned team hours each week. • The task-hour data are useful in improving team productivity.
Schedule plan	• The team produces a detailed schedule. • The team should also produce a Gantt chart for the project.
Earned-value plan	• The earned-value plan shows the rate of task completion. • The EV plan provides the basis for tracking team progress.
Team-member roles	• Each team member should have an assigned role. • Team roles cover items like quality, design, planning, or test.
Task plan	• The task plan shows the tasks that the team will work on and the hours that each task is expected to take. • The task plan also shows the earned value for completing each task and when that task is expected to be completed.

Table continued on next page.

Table C.2 Launch Products, *continued*

Product	Description
Detailed next-phase	The detailed next-phase plan shows what the team will do every week for the next several months.
Quality plan	• The team makes the quality plan. • This plan shows the expected defect levels at every process phase.
Risk evaluation	• The team's risk evaluation shows the principal risks. • Each risk is evaluated as to impact and likelihood.
Alternate plans	If the team's plan does not meet your goals, the team should present one or more alternate plans.

THE PLAN PRESENTATION

After reviewing the meeting agenda and describing the work that the team has done during the launch, the team leader will show a summary of the team's plan. In one example of such a presentation, Janet, the team leader, first described the team's strategy. She then showed the plan data in Figure C.2 and explained that the engineers made a detailed estimate of the planned product, defined the tasks to build this product, and estimated the time required for each task. (She could review the entire plan if you wished, but she plans to present only a summary of the plan data.) She explained that the plan schedule was 15 weeks longer than management had requested, but that the estimated total budget of 384 engineer weeks was slightly less than the planned project budget of 400 engineer weeks.

Since the plan did not meet management's goals, the team had examined several alternate plans, as shown in Figure C.3. The first alternate plan would require immediately adding two more PSP-trained engineers to the project. Since there were several such en-

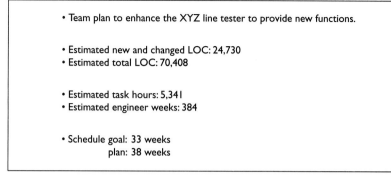

• Team plan to enhance the XYZ line tester to provide new functions.

• Estimated new and changed LOC: 24,730
• Estimated total LOC: 70,408

• Estimated task hours: 5,341
• Estimated engineer weeks: 384

• Schedule goal: 33 weeks
             plan: 38 weeks

Figure C.2 Project plan

gineers whose projects had not yet started, Janet suggested that two of them be assigned to this project, and that additional engineers be trained in the next scheduled PSP class. She also pointed out that adding these engineers would cut the schedule by ten weeks, which still would not meet management's goal. However, adding engineers would not increase the budgeted cost, because the total required engineer weeks would be the same in both cases.

Janet then explained that alternate 2 would meet management's 33-week goal and reduce budgeted costs by 12%. Since

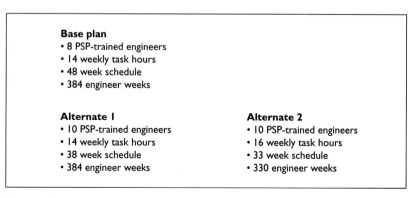

Base plan
• 8 PSP-trained engineers
• 14 weekly task hours
• 48 week schedule
• 384 engineer weeks

Alternate I
• 10 PSP-trained engineers
• 14 weekly task hours
• 38 week schedule
• 384 engineer weeks

Alternate 2
• 10 PSP-trained engineers
• 16 weekly task hours
• 33 week schedule
• 330 engineer weeks

Figure C.3 Alternate plans

this alternate required that the team achieve an average of 16 weekly task hours instead of the 14 in the plan, she planned first to discuss the task-hour problem as the team saw it. She explained that the engineers had planned only that part of their work that they could estimate and track, which included only the time to design, build, and test the product. These task hours did not include such other activities as coordinating with the hardware engineers, planning, team status meetings, meetings with management, and the many other things they had to do.

The engineers had talked to members of other TSP teams and found that 14 weekly task hours was an achievable goal but that 16 hours was much more difficult. However, they were willing to commit to the 16 task-hour objective if management agreed to the actions required. They expected to need some clerical support, an adjustment in working hours, and permission to work occasionally at home. They also wanted to block certain times of the week when they could work without interruption and when no meetings involving them would be called. They would develop more detailed recommendations in the next couple of weeks.

Janet next discussed the project risks, using the charts in Figures C.4 and C.5. Then she asked for questions and comments.

Risk 1: Team cannot average 16 task hours per week
• Likelihood: High
• Impact: High (5-week delay)

Mitigation: Weekly tracking plus management support with improvement actions

Risk 2: 2 additional PSP-trained engineers not available in time
• Likelihood: High
• Impact: High (10-week delay)

Mitigation: Identify trained engineers and get management priority to add to the project

---

Figure C.4 Major risks—1

Risk 3: System much larger than estimated
• Likelihood: Moderate
• Impact: High

Mitigation: Track program size and add resources if size grows and the schedule slips

Risk 4: Test hardware not available when needed
• Likelihood: Moderate
• Impact: High

Mitigation: Work with engineering on a backup testing plan

Figure C.5 Major risks—2

THE PLAN ASSESSMENT CHECKLIST

In probing the team's plan, your objective is to arrive at a realistic plan that the team will commit to and that meets business needs. A suggested set of questions to do this is given in the Plan Assessment Checklist in Table C.3. As shown in the checklist, your first questions should focus on the team's plan and alternate plans. If the team's plan is acceptable, then probe it to ensure that it is realistic and will produce a quality product. The Plan Assessment Checklist walks you through a set of questions to accomplish this objective.

THE BUSINESS ASSESSMENT

The first step in the assessment is to compare the team's plan with business needs. There are three general situations:

1. The team meets or exceeds the goal.
2. The team cannot meet the goal as planned, but could do so with more resources.
3. The team cannot meet the goal under any conditions.

Table C.3 The TSP Plan Assessment Checklist

Purpose	To guide your assessment of a TSP plan
Entry Criteria	The team has completed a TSP launch and has presented its plan.
General	• If the team has clear and factual answers, move quickly to the next item. • If the team is defensive or ill-prepared, ask more detailed questions. • Do not accept an incomplete or poor quality plan; have the team fix it. • Ask questions to understand the plan and to demonstrate interest.

Business Assessment

Step	Topics	Questions
1	Plan Assessment	• Does the plan or an alternate meet business needs? • Are the resource requirements acceptable? • If the plan has no acceptable plan, explore alternate strategies. • If you cannot identify an acceptable alternate plan, probe the team's plan to understand it. • If the plan is still unacceptable, thank the team, suspend the review, and hold a management meeting on next steps.

Plan Assessment

Step	Topics	Questions
2	Conceptual Design	• How confident is the team in the conceptual design? • Do the engineers have experience with similar systems?
3	The Size Estimate	• Is the size estimate based on historical data? • Has the team compared it with prior products?
4	Productivity	• Has the team compared the planned productivity with prior projects?

Plan Assessment	Evaluating the cost and schedule plan
Step	**Topics**	**Questions**
5	Weekly Task Hours	• How does the team's task-hour rate compare with prior experience? • Did the team use historical data to set the task-hour targets? • What actions can management take to help increase this rate?

Quality Assessment	Evaluating the quality plan
Step	**Topics**	**Questions**
6	Comparisons	• Has the team compared its quality plan with other team or industry data? • Does the team's quality plan set aggressive quality goals? • Are the test defect estimates realistic and has adequate time been allowed to find them?

Review Conclusion	Concluding the Plan Assessment
Step	**Topics**	**Questions**
7	Risk Assessment	• Was the team's risk assessment reasonably complete? • Has the team developed mitigation actions for the key risks?
8	Action Summary	• Has the team leader reviewed the meeting action items? • Does every action have an assigned responsibility?
9	Concluding Comments	Thank the participants for their contributions and congratulate them on the work they have done.

Exit Criteria	
	• The plan was reviewed and approved or the team told how to change it. • The actions items have been defined and assigned.

The Team Meets or Exceeds the Goal

If the team's plan meets the goal and you feel the plan is reasonably accurate and realistic, proceed to the rest of the plan assessment. In the example, the team produced a 48-week schedule as opposed to the desired 33 weeks. In this case, the engineers produced two alternate plans, one of which met management needs and was accepted.

The Team Needs Added Resources

As in the case of Janet's project, the most common situation is that the team could meet management's desired schedule, but only with added resources. Assuming the engineers presented an alternative plan that showed what they could do with more people, they have done their job and you must make a decision. You can either add the needed resources, proceed on the longer schedule, or explore other alternatives.

If the team has not presented an alternate plan to meet your goals, ask why not. Is there some reason that additional resources would not help, or did the engineers not think to make an alternate plan? Teams generally can accelerate schedules by adding resources, but the added resources must be properly trained and available in time. If the alternate plan is satisfactory and you and the project managers agree that the needed resources can be obtained, move on to the rest of the plan assessment.

The Team Cannot Meet the Goal

Occasionally, teams will not see how to meet the business need. Presumably, they will have produced the best plan that they could devise and have presented it to you for approval. At this point, you should carefully examine the team's plan to see if there are any variations that might meet the business need. If so, have the team produce a suitable alternative plan.

If you cannot think of an alternative approach that would likely meet the business needs, examine the engineers' plan to make sure it is realistic and properly made. If problems exist that, if corrected, will likely make the plan acceptable, have the team take the time to correct the plan and review it with management again. If no acceptable alternatives appear likely, thank the engineers for their work, conclude the review, and hold a separate management meeting to reassess the business needs and decide what to do.

THE PLAN ASSESSMENT

After you have concluded that the team's plan or an alternate plan will meet your needs, review that plan carefully to ensure that it was made professionally and that it adequately represents the work to be done. The remainder of the plan assessment process follows the general strategy shown in Figure C.6.

As shown in Figure C.6, the planning process starts with the conceptual design, which in turn determines the size estimate. Based on the size estimate and historical productivity data, the team can estimate the task hours for the development work. Similarly, the size estimate, together with the team's quality plan, determines how many defects must be removed in testing and how many task hours will be required for that testing. With the development and testing task hours, together with the team's weekly task-hour plan, the team can produce the schedule. This suggests that the conceptual design be the first item to examine, followed by the size estimate, the productivity estimate, and the quality plan.

The Conceptual Design

In making a TSP plan, teams first estimate the sizes of the products they will build and then use productivity data to determine

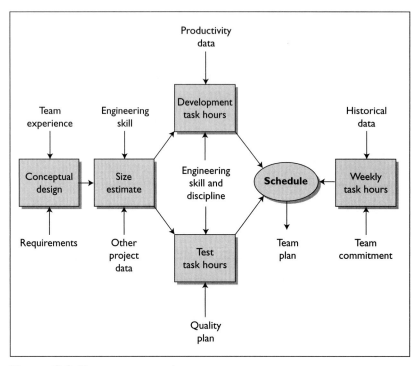

Figure C.6 Plan assessment elements

how long the work will take. Before they can estimate the sizes of the products, however, they must have some idea of what the products will look like. Then they must determine the product structure and define its principal components. Because teams do not have time to produce a full product design during the launch, they must produce a conceptual design. This conceptual design represents the team's current thinking about how to design and build the product. The engineers then use this conceptual design as the basis for making the size estimate.

You need not assess the conceptual design itself, but you should ask the engineers how comfortable they are with the design. If it is similar to other designs that the engineers have worked on, it will be reasonably good. If only a few of the engineers have worked on similar products, however, the conceptual design is likely to contain errors and omissions. Then there is a reasonable chance that the job will be significantly larger and take longer than planned. When engineers have not worked with similar systems, they often omit key functions or assume that important functions are simpler than they turn out to be.

The Size Estimate

After discussing the conceptual design, ask about the size estimate. Did the engineers compare this size estimate with similar prior products? Even if only two or three of the engineers have worked on similar products, if they used historical data to make the estimate and they feel confident about the estimate, the estimates for each of the system parts are probably pretty accurate.

The Productivity Estimate

Ask how the team's planned productivity compares with the engineers' experience, both in the PSP course and with other projects. In the TSP, overall productivity is measured in LOC per hour for the total job. What did the engineers use for productivity numbers, and where did they get those numbers? Engineering productivity for complete TSP projects usually is between one and ten LOC per task hour.

One important factor to consider in assessing team productivity is that new development work typically has higher productivity than modification or enhancement. Also, the development productivity for more complex communications or systems control programs generally falls at the low end of the productivity range, while application development work usually has higher productivity.

The Task-Hour Measure

Since variations in the weekly task-hour rate can have a major impact on project cost and schedule, thoroughly explore the basis for the weekly task-hour estimate. As Janet explained in the example, in a normal 40-hour work week, engineers do many things other than designing, coding, and testing. These other tasks can take a great deal of time, and every minute spent on these activities is a minute that the engineers cannot spend on developing the product.

If this is a first-time TSP team, these task hours should probably average about 10 hours in the first few weeks and then gradually build up to about 14 to 16 task hours per week. Further increases generally require a long-term improvement program. Until teams have historical data, it is risky to plan for more than this. When teams pick larger numbers, they frequently fall behind schedule and have trouble recovering. In reviewing the task-hour plan, ask about the data that the engineers used to make the plan. Do they have prior data on their own work, on the organization, or on similar teams in other organizations? If so, how do their planned task hours compare with these other teams, and what assumptions did they make in picking the task-hour rate for this project?

Once the organization has task-hour data, management should consider ways to help the team improve its weekly task hours. Remember, however, that the task-hour rate is a motivational issue. Management edicts to improve weekly task hours usually are counterproductive. Focus on what management can do to help the engineers improve their own task time. The engineers know that their weekly task hours are important, so trust them to set their own goals and help them to achieve these goals.

AN EXAMPLE PLAN COMPARISON

Janet's project illustrates the kinds of comparative plan data that team leaders should show. In answer to management's questions, she showed the chart in Figure C.7 and explained that the organization had historical data on only three projects. Although these were not TSP data, several of the team members had worked on these projects and felt that the numbers reasonably represented what happened. She had also talked to finance and obtained the working hours and engineer week data.

Based on these comparisons, it appears that the team's project plan is very aggressive. From the LOC/week numbers, productivity is about 50% higher than two of the projects and nearly three times that of the third. Since the team's project was a large and relatively stand-alone addition to an existing application, Janet believed that the higher productivity was realistic. She also pointed out that project B consisted of many small coding changes in a large system; this is the least productive kind of software work.

Since these plan numbers look very aggressive, management should be concerned about an overcommitment and an exposed

		Projects		
	Plan	A	B	C
New and changed KLOC	24.7	38	12	71
Task hours	5,341			
Working hours	15,360	31,600	18,300	51,700
LOC/working hour	1.62	1.20	0.66	1.37
Calendar weeks	33	71	16	118
Engineer weeks	330	790	458	1,293
LOC/engineer week	74.9	48.1	26.2	54.9

Figure C.7 Plan comparisons

schedule. Without better historical data, however, there is no good way to tell. One approach is to accept this plan for now and to watch carefully in case the estimate is too low. If it turns out to be too low, management might have to add more PSP-trained engineers to the project or accept a later delivery.

EVALUATING THE QUALITY PLAN

There are three reasons to ask about the quality plan. First, your interest in quality will send the right message. Emphasize that the quality of the engineers' work is more important than the schedule. Second, the quality of the work will have a direct impact on the schedule. If some engineers do poor-quality design or implementation work, the entire team will waste time in finding and fixing the resulting defects. Third, quality is important to the business. For poor-quality products, field repair and warranty costs often exceed development costs. Every defect that a customer finds costs time and money and damages your reputation. While you need not examine the quality plan itself, you should ask questions about it.

Continuing with the previous example, in answer to the questions on quality, Janet showed the chart in Figure C.8. She pointed out that this was the organization's first TSP project, so none of the other projects had comparable quality data. Therefore, she compared the team's plan with the TSP quality guidelines, which provide quality goals for teams to use when they do not have other project data.

Janet next explained that the team planned to find 68.7 total defects/KLOC. This might seem like a large number, but actually it was below the quality guideline range of 75 to 150. Even with this low total defect density, however, the total number of defects to be found and fixed during development was 1,700. By using thorough reviews and inspections, the team planned to

	Plan	Guideline
Defects/KLOC		
Total development	68.7	75–150
System test	0.23	0.20
Acceptance test	0.10	
Product life	0.24	
Defects removed	**Plan**	
Total development	1,700	
Code reviews	723	
Unit test	23.3	
System test	5.6	
Acceptance test	2.5	
Post development	5.9	
Process yield	**Plan**	**Guideline**
% before unit test	97.3	85+
% before system test	99.2	99+
Final test as % of development	4.6%	
(typical values are around 50%)		

Figure C.8 The quality plan

remove 97.3% of these defects before the first unit tests. This would result in 5.6 defects to be found in system test, and another 8.4 (2.5 + 5.9 = 8.4) defects left in the product at delivery. Finally, Janet explained that yield before system test was very important. If, like most projects, the team achieved a yield before system test of only 80% to 90%, the engineers would have to spend another 2,000 to 3,000 hours in testing.

ASSESSING THE PLAN

After reviewing these items, you should be able to judge the quality of the team's cost, schedule, and quality plans. If the plans were thorough and the engineers' answers were clear and logical, compliment them and move on to the risk assessment. However, if the engineers have not used available data, consulted resident experts, or built on prior work, thank them for what they have done but ask them to take more time to finish the job.

The plan provides the foundation for everything the team will do. If inaccurate or incomplete, it will not provide useful guidance. Using a poor plan is like driving a car with a broken gas gauge: you might not run out of gas right away, but the longer you drive, the greater your risk. By having the engineers fix the plan, you establish the principle that you will not accept incomplete or incorrect work. Standards start at the top, so to consistently get quality work, start by insisting on a properly made and complete plan.

EXAMINING THE TEAM'S RISK ASSESSMENT

Once you have assessed the team's cost, schedule, and quality plans, ask about the risk assessment. The team has evaluated the risks that the engineers think are most significant and presented a few of them to you. You will not want to review all these risks, but check that the major risks have been considered and that the team has identified where it needs help.

MEETING CONCLUSION

After your questions have been answered, thank the team leader and team members for their work and congratulate them on what they have accomplished. Also say a few words about the challenges ahead, and explain that you are counting on the engineers to do a superior job. Finally, conclude with a clear and concise statement of your decision on the team's plan and a quick review of any required follow-up actions. The team leader will then close the meeting by having the meeting recorder read the outstanding action items, the person assigned to handle each item, and the follow-up date.

SUMMARY

The following eight principal points are made in this appendix:

1. When the engineers have completed the TSP launch, they will present their plan in a final management meeting.

2. An executive or senior manager must attend this meeting.

3. The purpose of the plan review is to convince you that the team has made a thorough and realistic plan for doing the job.

4. Follow the Plan Assessment Checklist to review the team's plan.

5. In doing this review, ask about the conceptual design, size estimate, productivity estimate, quality plan, and risk assessment.

6. By doing a thorough review, you satisfy yourself that the plan was made competently and you require the engineers to defend it.

7. Once the engineers have defended their plan and you have accepted it, they will be highly motivated to meet their commitment to you.

8. Close the review with a brief summary of your decision about the plan and a review of the outstanding action items.

D

The Quarterly Project Review

O nce you have built a capable software organization, you need to maintain it. If you don't, this capability will almost certainly deteriorate, and probably very quickly. The quarterly project review is an effective way to maintain a strong software capability. In the review process, you examine the status of the major projects at least once every three months. When your organization is just starting to use the TSP, review the projects every month or so. Once the projects are functioning properly, you can move to quarterly reviews.

This appendix describes why quarterly project reviews are important and how to conduct them. It also provides a review checklist, a review strategy, and some examples of the issues you are likely to encounter.

WHY YOU SHOULD HOLD REVIEWS

As an executive, your principal objective is to use business assets to take advantage of strategic opportunities. You will need a capable and effective engineering organization, and for this you will need a capable and effective software operation. To know that your software work is done competently, you must know where the projects stand and how these projects are being run.

You also need to assess project and program management. Quarterly reviews will help you to do this.

Another reason to hold periodic reviews is to help the engineers do better work. Quality work requires discipline, and discipline requires coaching and management support. By holding periodic reviews, you maintain management's focus on the way the teams are performing their work. The reasons that reviews help you do this are as follows:

1. To produce quality products on schedule and for planned costs, the engineers must consistently follow disciplined practices.

2. To consistently follow disciplined practices, the engineers need to know that management cares about the quality of their work.

3. To demonstrate concern about quality, the managers must examine the work regularly and insist that the engineers use disciplined practices.

4. To sustain your emphasis on quality, the managers must know that software quality is important to you.

5. The quarterly project review is an effective way to demonstrate that you care about the quality of the software work.

REVIEW CONSIDERATIONS

In reviewing projects, executives often do more harm than good. The two principal areas of concern are schedule management and team motivation. Executives are prone to setting aggressive schedule goals and insisting that their dates be met. Unless they have engineering experience, they often fail to appreciate the negative impact that unreasonably tight schedules can have on an engineering team.

Schedule Management

When most managers review a project, they only ask about the schedule. This is a mistake for two reasons. First, the actual date when the job will be completed is primarily determined by the scope of the job, the date the work started, the resources applied, and the quality of the engineers' work. Second, when managers push engineers to complete work quickly, the engineers rush through the tasks, make many mistakes, and spend more time fixing problems than they would have spent doing the job correctly. Excessive pressure extends schedules by months and often years.

By concentrating on the schedule, managers overlook the things they can influence. These are to start jobs promptly, provide adequate staffing, and ensure that the work is done in a disciplined and professional way.

Team Motivation

Getting engineers to follow disciplined practices is a motivational issue. While managers must emphasize the importance of disciplined practices, any attempt to coerce or demand disciplined behavior will not be effective. There are five elements to motivating disciplined engineering behavior.

First, if the job is bigger than expected, reset the goals. Driving teams to meet unreasonable goals builds losing teams. Make a new strategy, reset the plan, and get the team on a winning track. The engineers will feel better about their jobs, and they will do better work.

Second, people most often achieve challenging goals when they have enthusiastic support. When teams are winning and the crowd is cheering, everything seems to work. The performers are energized, enthusiastic, and striving to break new records. So focus on success. Compliment the engineers on what they have accomplished. Emphasize their achievements and concentrate on building a winning team.

Third, consistently disciplined work requires coaching and support. Even when properly trained, and even with strong management support, engineers will not routinely follow disciplined personal practices. It is not that they are uncooperative but that disciplined behavior is difficult. Few people can maintain discipline without guidance and support. That is why sports professionals and performing artists have coaches, conductors, and directors.

Fourth, the engineers must know how to do disciplined work, and they must believe they are more productive when they do. Establishing and maintaining such beliefs takes training, experience, and continued management reinforcement. Provide the engineers with the proper training. If you don't, they won't be able to do disciplined or quality work regardless of their motivation and commitment.

And last, the engineers' managers must recognize the importance of disciplined work. They must view disciplined behavior as a required part of the job. If you and your managers truly believe that it is always faster and cheaper to do the job in a planned and disciplined way, motivating disciplined behavior will not be difficult.

If you concentrate on providing adequate trained resources and motivating disciplined work, your reviews will be rewarding for you and for your people.

THE REVIEW STRATEGY

In assessing the performance of TSP teams, it is relatively easy to determine the status of the projects against their plans. The detail of TSP plans and their earned-value and task-time methods provide precise status measures. With these measures, you will also know the team's rate of progress and can tell to within days when the engineers will finish the job.

This degree of predictability would be a major step for most software organizations, but it is merely a first step. To achieve an effective software capability, you need to assess the engineers' work in terms of performance stages:

- The common stage: Teams are performing pretty much as they always have. The first step in moving from the common to the initial stage is to train the engineers in the PSP and to launch their teams under the guidance of trained TSP coaches.

- The initial stage: The engineers have been trained in the PSP, their teams have been launched with the TSP, and they have started to track their time, calculate their earned-value, and report their task-time data. The initial-stage review ensures that teams are starting to use PSP and TSP practices properly and that they are following their defined process and plan.

- The standard stage: Teams are planning, tracking, and reporting on their work, as well as measuring and managing the quality of their products. The principal challenge at the standard stage is for teams to record and use their defect data. Once they do this, benchmarked improvement is possible.

This suggests the following review strategy:

1. Once the engineers have been trained and their teams launched, focus first on the initial stage. Are the engineers following their plans, tracking and recording time, measuring task hours, and reporting earned-value progress? If not, find out why and get these problems fixed before

moving to the standard-stage topics. As soon as several team members are doing these things, move on to the standard-stage review.

2. At the standard stage, your initial focus should be on defect data. Are the engineers recording all the defect data? If not, get that problem fixed before asking more questions about quality.

3. In asking about defects, remember that the data are sensitive. Do not say anything that implies criticism of the engineers. This topic is covered in more detail in Appendix E.

4. Once the teams have made a good start on gathering defect data, ask about the quality metrics. Stress the importance of good defect data and ask about yields, defect levels, defect ratios, and time ratios. Ask how these measures compare with the plan, the TSP guidelines, or the benchmarked TSP teams.

5. In subsequent reviews, look at trends. Where is the team improving and where are there problems? Have the team set both short- and long-term improvement goals, and see what management can do to help.

Conclude the review by asking for specific commitments. Where teams are not following plans or gathering time and size data, have them describe the improvements they will make before the next review. Once teams meet the basic planning and tracking criteria, ask about defect data and quality. Then move on to benchmarked improvement. Where do the team's measures fall short, what are the next improvement steps, and what short-term goals has the team set? Also ask what the team plans to show you at the next review. Have the commitments documented, and their status reported as the first item in the next review. If you conduct such regular quarterly reviews, your teams will soon be measuring and managing the quality of their work.

The rest of this appendix and Appendix E describe how to conduct reviews and suggest questions to ask.

THE REVIEW PROCESS

Your principal objective in doing a project review is to determine how the work is being done. Since the TSP provides the data needed to measure project status, the team should be able to make a status presentation with little or no preparation. However, the team leader will almost certainly prepare a special presentation. Your objective in asking questions is to find out how this team is actually performing. That generally will require at least some questions that the team does not expect.

While there are many ways to conduct reviews, it is usually helpful to follow a defined process. This makes the reviews more efficient and helps to ensure that they are complete. The Quarterly Review Checklist in Table D.1 suggests the questions and the order in which to ask them. You should follow this checklist fairly closely at first, but feel free to modify it as you gain experience with reviews.

WHEN TO HOLD THE FIRST REVIEW

Hold the first project review a month or two after the project launch, but give the engineers time to start the job. Too early a review will expose issues that the engineers should solve for themselves. While new TSP teams will have many questions, the coach can handle most of them without management help. After a month or two, the engineers will have answered their initial questions and gathered some early data. The objective of the first review is to make sure the teams are following the process.

Table D.1 The Quarterly Review Checklist

Purpose	• To guide executives and senior managers in conducting project reviews • To motivate the engineers to do superior work
Entry Criteria	• All of the engineers have been PSP trained and the teams were launched under the guidance of a trained TSP coach. • The team has worked for at least a month since the TSP launch. • The executive or senior manager is familiar with the TSP process and has been given a copy of this checklist.
General	• The team leader leads the review, presents status, and answers questions. • If practical, invite the team members to attend the review. • Repeat the initial questions (1–8) until the results are satisfactory. • As soon as the engineers are tracking time and earned value, move to questions 9–15. • Once some engineers are tracking and using defect data, start asking about benchmarked improvement (question 16).

Step	Activities	Review Questions
1	Planning	• Do the engineers have detailed plans, and are they following these plans? • Do these plans follow the defined team process? • Are the plans sufficiently detailed to guide the work?
2	Task Time	• Are the team's weekly task hours near or above the plan? • If not, are actions planned to improve the weekly task-hour rate?
3	Earned Value	• Is the team tracking earned value? • If EV is below the plan, has the team planned actions to recover?
4	Completion Projections	• Do the team's schedule projections indicate problems? • Has the team planned actions to address these problems?
5	Load Balancing	Is the team rebalancing its workload whenever necessary?

Step	Activities	Review Questions
6	Time Recording	Are the engineers using the time recording log to record their time?
7	Task Recording	Are the engineers recording when they complete each project task?
8	Size Recording	Are the engineers properly recording their size data?
9	Defect Recording	• Are the engineers properly recording their defect data? • Are they using the defect recording log?
10	Reviews	• Is the team conducting all of the required reviews and inspections? • Are the engineers using and updating their personal review checklists?
11	Review Rates	Is the team meeting its review rate plan?
12	Ratios	Is the team meeting its phase and defect ratio plans?
13	Yield	Is the team meeting its phase and process yield plan?
14	Defect Density	Is the team meeting its defect density plan?
15	Test Defects	• Is the team's estimate of final test defects reasonable? • Is the planned test time adequate for finding these defects?
16	Benchmarks	How does the team's performance compare with the benchmark teams?
17	Management Actions	At the conclusion of the review • Summarize the actions to be taken. • Verify that the team leader will write a brief review report. • If management actions are needed, check that responsibility is assigned. • Summarize the improvements you will look for in the next review. • Compliment the team and the team leader for the work they have done.
Exit Criteria		• The appropriate review stage topics have been covered. • Action items have been defined, reviewed, and assigned. • The meeting report responsibility has been assigned.

In later reviews, you can judge whether the team's plan is realistic or if changes are required.

The following paragraphs illustrate the questions to ask TSP teams and the answers you will likely get. The examples also illustrate some of the information that is potentially available on TSP projects.

THE INITIAL-STAGE REVIEW

To show how an initial-stage review is conducted, we will again use Janet's project, after the team has completed four weeks of work. In describing project status, she shows the data in Figures D.1, D.2, D.3, and D.4. Janet first explains that the team completed the launch ahead of time so the engineers are slightly ahead of their schedule for the requirements tasks. They are now starting system test planning and the requirements inspections. However, she is concerned about the EV projection in Figure D.2. It indicates that the project will complete eight weeks late.

Janet then shows the weekly report form in Figure D.4 and explains that the team is behind on earned value (EV)* to date with an actual value of 7.3 as opposed to the plan of 8.9. Using the weekly data, she points out two problems: the project hours are behind plan and the engineers are taking longer to complete tasks than planned. From the last line in the weekly data section of Figure D.4, she shows that the completed tasks have taken 421 hours, compared with the plan of 380 hours. This 11% overrun would be serious if it continued for the rest of the project.

---

* Earned value measures a team's progress against its plan. Each task's planned value (PV) equals that task's planned percentage of the total job. When that task is completed, the project earns that value (EV).

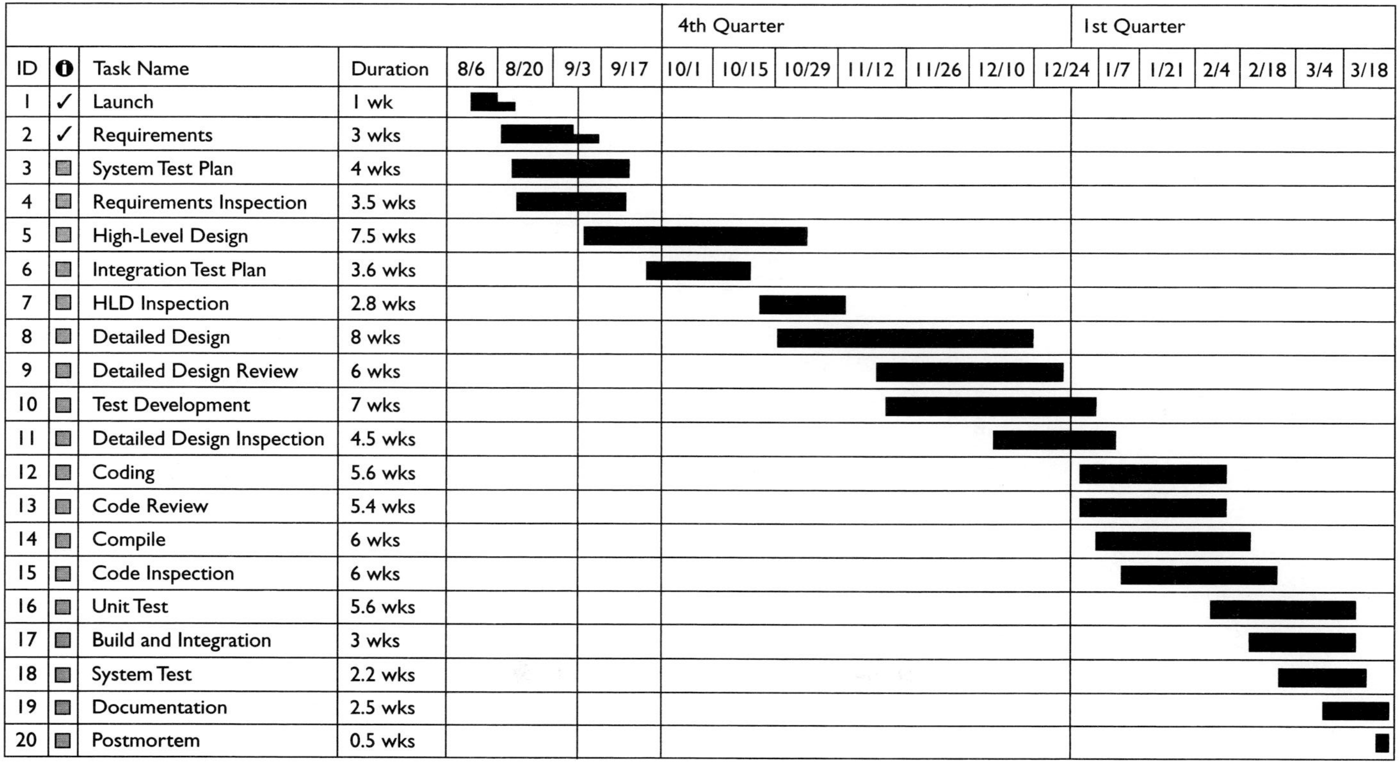

ID	●	Task Name	Duration
1	✓	Launch	1 wk
2	✓	Requirements	3 wks
3		System Test Plan	4 wks
4		Requirements Inspection	3.5 wks
5		High-Level Design	7.5 wks
6		Integration Test Plan	3.6 wks
7		HLD Inspection	2.8 wks
8		Detailed Design	8 wks
9		Detailed Design Review	6 wks
10		Test Development	7 wks
11		Detailed Design Inspection	4.5 wks
12		Coding	5.6 wks
13		Code Review	5.4 wks
14		Compile	6 wks
15		Code Inspection	6 wks
16		Unit Test	5.6 wks
17		Build and Integration	3 wks
18		System Test	2.2 wks
19		Documentation	2.5 wks
20		Postmortem	0.5 wks

Date scale (left to right): 8/6, 8/20, 9/3, 9/17 | 4th Quarter: 10/1, 10/15, 10/29, 11/12, 11/26, 12/10, 12/24 | 1st Quarter: 1/7, 1/21, 2/4, 2/18, 3/4, 3/18

Figure D.1 Project status—4 weeks

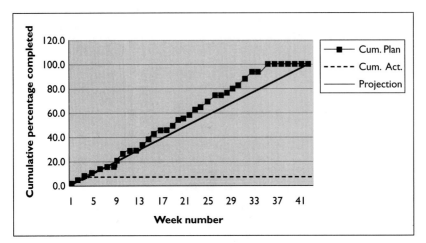

Figure D.2 Project earned value—4-week actual

Questions on Planning

In following the Quarterly Review Checklist, first ask about the team's plan. Is it sufficiently detailed to guide the engineers' work, and does it reflect what the engineers are actually doing? Does the

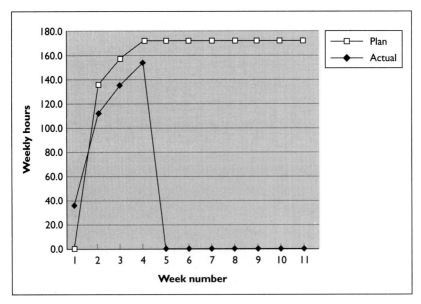

Figure D.3 Weekly task hours—4-week actual

TSP Week Summary—Form WEEK

Name _____   Date 8/11/2001
Team _____
Status for Week [4]   Cycle 1

Weekly Data	Plan	Actual	Plan/ Actual
Project hours for this week	170.0	153.1	1.11
Project hours this cycle to date	462.0	436.2	1.06
Earned value for this week	1.9	4.6	0.41
Earned value this cycle to date	8.9	7.3	1.22
To-date hours for tasks completed	380.0	421.8	0.90

Assembly	Plan Hours	Actual Hours	Earned Value	Planned Week	Plan Hrs./ Actual Hrs.
Requirements elicitation	57.0	56.3	1.1	2	1.01
Requirements analysis	55.0	61.0	1.1	3	0.90
Requirements evaluation	101.0	144.1	1.9	3	0.70
Requirements draft	70.0	94.2	1.3	4	0.74
Requirements documentation	67.0	38.0	1.3	5	1.76
System test requirements	30.0	28.2	0.6	6	1.06

Figure D.4 The week form

team plan follow its defined process, does it include inspection and review steps, and do the engineers have the training and skills to handle the tasks they have been assigned? Typical planning problems concern underestimates, unplanned tasks, or skill problems. Also, teams often start with incomplete or inaccurate requirements and must take time to correct them. An early indication of this problem is requirements tasks that take longer than planned. This is the case with Janet's team.

Questions on Task Time

In explaining the impact of the team's weekly task-hour problem, Janet points to Figure D.3. The engineers have been below the plan for the last three weeks, but their task-hour rate is improving. Although the team is running about 18% behind on EV to date, Janet believes there is still time to correct the problem. The engineers have also suggested actions to improve their weekly task hours:

1. Establish morning quiet times when the engineers would not answer their phones, there would be no meetings, and the team members would not be disturbed.

2. Work at home two days a week.

3. Get clerical support to handle supplies, make copies, do typing, or do any other miscellaneous chores that will save the engineers time.

4. Work on Saturday and take off Monday.

5. Come in late two mornings and work later in the evening.

Questions on Earned Value

As shown in Table D.2, the relationship between earned value and task hours can tell you a great deal about a project. Depending on the situation, try to understand the team's problems and what management can do to help. Ask what the engineers see as the problems and use the team's data to interpret the answers. Janet's project appears to be case 5 in Table D.2. In discussing the EV problem, Janet points to the completion projection in Figure D.2. This shows that, at the present rate of progress, the project will be completed in 41 weeks instead of the planned 33 weeks.

Completion Projections

Janet explains that the project has an 8-week schedule exposure because the team had earned 7.30 EV in the first three weeks, for

Table D.2 Interpreting Earned-Value and Task-Time Data

Task hours/Earned value	EV on plan	EV < plan	EV > plan
Task hours on plan	1. The project is on plan with no obvious problems.	4. This situation is probably caused by an underestimate.	7. The team is working faster than planned or is not spending enough time on some tasks.
Task hours < plan	2. The team has either overestimated the job or is not spending enough time on some tasks.	5. This situation is probably caused by low task hours.	8. As in 7, the team is working faster than planned or is not spending enough time on some tasks.
Task hours > plan	3. The team has underestimated the job and is putting in more task hours than planned.	6. As in 4, this situation is probably caused by an underestimate.	9. The team is doing more work than planned and is ahead of schedule.

an average weekly rate of 2.43 EV.* At this rate, the project would reach 100 EV (and finish the job) at 41 weeks (100/2.43 = 41.15). However, because it is still early and the team's task-hour rate is improving, she believes the team can recover.

Questions on Load-Balancing

In answer to your questions on workload balancing, Janet explains that the engineers are still following the plan they developed during the launch, but their workload distribution is becoming unbalanced. She hopes to use the current plan until the relaunch in about two months but will watch the situation carefully. If necessary, they will take half a day to update the plan and rebalance the workload.

Questions on Time Recording

In answer to your questions on time recording, Janet believes that the engineers are recording their time properly but has not looked at their time-recording logs. She will do so right away. If any engineers are recording time data once a day or once a week, she agrees that these data would not be accurate enough for managing the project.

Questions on Size Recording

Janet did not have size data at the 4-week review, but she did at the 17-week review three months later. In answer to your questions on size recording, she shows Figure D.5 and explains that the plan line shows the team's original estimate of 24,730 KLOC, with updates for the completed modules. As each module is unit tested, the actual size measures are substituted for the estimates. The estimated total line shows a linear extrapolation

---

* Note that the team earned no EV in week 1 during the TSP launch, so the 7.3 EV was earned in three weeks.

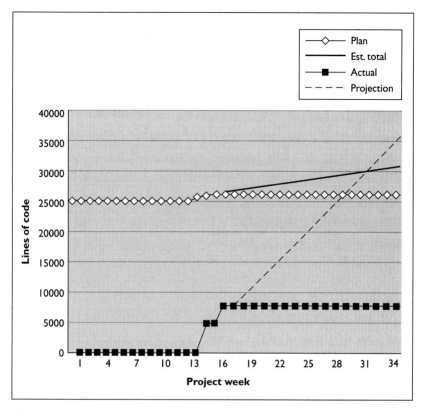

Figure D.5 Line-of-code projections

of the growth in the total size estimate as components are completed. She also explains that the lines at the bottom of the figure show the actual sizes of the coded and unit tested modules, together with a linear projection of the actual size data.

By projecting the plan and actual size data, she can judge how big the system will be and when they will complete coding and unit testing. This is when the plan and actual size lines intersect—at 32 weeks. Here, the size value is about 30,000 LOC—indicating that the finished product size will be about 30,000 LOC instead of the original estimate of 24,730 LOC. It also suggests that the coding and unit testing will be completed at 32 weeks. Since they plan only 3 weeks of work after the last unit test, this indicates about a 2-week schedule exposure. While still a concern, this is a substantial improvement over the 8-week exposure she reported in the first quarterly review.

STANDARD-STAGE REVIEWS

This team is doing a reasonable job of making and following its plan, although the data-gathering situation is not yet clear. If, at the next review, Janet reports that the engineers are properly gathering the time and size data, you can move on to the standard-stage review questions. These questions are discussed in Appendix E.

SUMMARY AND CONCLUSIONS

The following eight principal points are made in this appendix:

1. The objective of the quarterly review is to motivate teams to do their best work.

2. Hold the first project review about one to two months after the project has been launched.

3. In conducting the review, use the TSP Quarterly Review Checklist.

4. TSP reviews are conducted in stages, with the initial-stage reviews first concentrating on planning and tracking.

5. If necessary, repeat the initial-stage questions until the results are satisfactory.

6. Once at least some of the engineers have demonstrated competence at the initial stage, move on to the standard-stage questions. These questions are discussed in Appendix E.

7. At the end of the review, ask for a summary of the actions to be taken, and verify that someone is assigned to each action item.

8. Close the meeting by summarizing the principal topics that you will explore in the next review, and thank the team and team leader for their efforts.

E

The Standard-Stage Review

This appendix describes standard-stage reviews and contains examples of the issues that you are likely to encounter in conducting them. These reviews are part of the quarterly project review process described in Appendix D.

Once your teams have passed the initial-stage review, they usually will meet schedules and accurately report project status. The next challenge is for them to consistently deliver quality products. Once schedules are under control, the typical executive's reaction is to view the software problem as solved and to move on to other more pressing areas. Although you can certainly reduce the time that you devote to software issues, you should not stop doing quarterly project reviews.

Quality work requires discipline, and discipline is hard to maintain. By holding periodic reviews, you sustain everyone's focus on quality. Without your continued interest, the managers are likely to concentrate on your current priorities and stop reviewing their projects or asking about quality. If this single-minded focus on schedule continues for long, the teams will stop measuring and tracking the quality of their work, and soon they will stop following the TSP process altogether. Then software engineering performance will deteriorate and you will be right back where you started: wondering how to get faster, better, cheaper software work.

To repeat what we said in Appendix D, the reasons reviews help to maintain a focus on quality are as follows:

1. To produce quality products on schedule and for planned costs, the engineers must consistently follow disciplined practices.
2. To consistently follow disciplined practices, the engineers need to know that management cares about the quality of their work.
3. To demonstrate concern about quality, the managers must examine the work regularly and insist that the engineers use disciplined practices.
4. To sustain your emphasis on quality, the managers must know that software quality is important to you.
5. The quarterly project review is an effective way to demonstrate that you care about the quality of the software work.

YIELD MANAGEMENT

With any kind of hardware or software work, the most effective quality strategy is to strive for quality products before testing begins. That is the only way to consistently get quality products out of test. To manage software quality this way, the focus must be on yield management. Here, *yield* is the percentage of defects removed in a test, an inspection, or a review. Think about the defect-removal process as a series of filters. Each filter removes a percentage of the defects in a program. The percentage removed by each filtration step is called the yield of that filter.

An example of how this filtering process works is shown in Figure E1. Here, the Jet Propulsion Laboratory (JPL) found 186 defects during the system testing of the Magellan spacecraft [1]. This system had only 22,000 LOC, but testing took more than two years. One reason testing took so much time is that the critical defects were found in bursts, with a burst only after some number of noncritical defects was first found and fixed. Because defects can mask other defects, testing can take a very long time. This example also illustrates how ineffective testing can be at producing quality products. Even after over two years of system testing, the Magellan mission was still plagued with software problems.

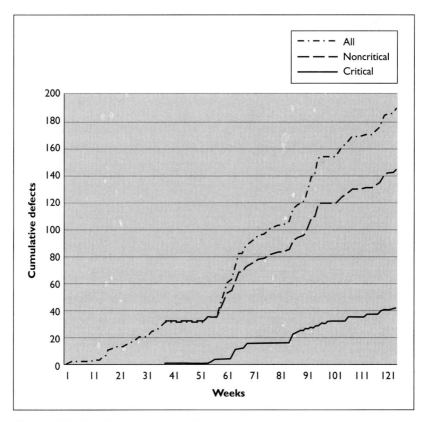

Figure E.1 Magellan system test defects

Since most projects have tight schedules, engineers will stop testing when they think they have found most of the defects. From these Magellan data, few defects were found from weeks 3 through 10 and then again from weeks 37 through 51. Had JPL stopped after the first year of testing, there still would have been 40 critical defects left in the spacecraft. Then, instead of being a troubled mission, it would likely have failed completely.

REVIEW CONSIDERATIONS

To perform effectively, TSP teams must plan, track, and report on their work, and they must measure and manage the quality of their products. The principal challenge at the standard stage is to have teams record and use their defect data. Once they consistently do this, benchmarked improvement is possible. The standard-stage review strategy is as follows:

1. At the standard stage, the first focus is on defect data. If few of the engineers are recording defect data, fix that problem before asking more quality questions.

2. Remember that defect data are sensitive.

3. Once many team members are consistently gathering defect data, ask about quality metrics.

4. In subsequent reviews, look at trends. Where is the team improving, and where do the engineers still have problems? Have them set short- and long-term improvement goals, and ask what management can do to help them continue improving.

5. To set more aggressive goals, use other teams or other organizations as benchmarks.

6. Always conclude a review by asking for specific actions and commitments.

The rest of this appendix contains more detailed guidance on conducting standard-stage reviews. It also includes suggested questions to ask. In this discussion, we will again use the Quarterly Review Checklist introduced in Appendix D. It is shown again in Table E.1. Plan to follow this checklist fairly closely at first, but feel free to modify it as you gain experience with reviews.

DEFECT RECORDING

The first objective of the standard-stage review is to determine if the engineers are recording data on their defects. If not, management needs to motivate them to do so—and do it in a way that is not critical or threatening. These defect data are required to assess the quality of the development process and to manage product quality. Therefore, an important objective of the standard-stage review is to ensure that the engineers' defect data are accurate and complete.

Since injecting defects is human, it is important to motivate engineers to find them. The objective is to leave as few defects as possible in the product at the end of each development phase. To keep these defect numbers in perspective, 5 defects per KLOC would be considered poor quality in a delivered product. However, when you consider that the printed listing of a 1,000 LOC (or 1 KLOC) program takes about 20 pages of text, 5 errors in 20 pages of typing is better than just about any newspaper, magazine, or book, and certainly better than typical office correspondence. Even poor-quality software has higher quality than any other manually produced product.

Since the defect data are gathered by the engineers on their personal mistakes and there is no other way to gather the data, the completeness and accuracy of these data depend entirely on the engineers. Remember that every defect is caused by an engineer's

Table E.1 The Quarterly Review Checklist

Purpose	• To guide executives and senior managers in conducting project reviews • To motivate the engineers to do superior work
Entry Criteria	• All of the engineers have been PSP trained and the teams were launched under the guidance of a trained TSP coach. • The team has worked for at least a month since the TSP launch. • The executive or senior manager is familiar with the TSP process and has been given a copy of this checklist.
General	• The team leader leads the review, presents status, and answers questions. • If practical, invite the team members to attend the review. • Repeat the initial questions (1–8) until the results are satisfactory. • As soon as the engineers are tracking time and earned value, move to questions 9–15. • Once some engineers are tracking and using defect data, start asking about benchmarked improvement (question 16).

Step	Activities	Review Questions
1	Planning	• Do the engineers have detailed plans, and are they following these plans? • Do these plans follow the defined team process? • Are the plans sufficiently detailed to guide the work?
2	Task Time	• Are the team's weekly task hours near or above the plan? • If not, are actions planned to improve the weekly task-hour rate?
3	Earned Value	• Is the team tracking earned value? • If EV is below the plan, has the team planned actions to recover?
4	Completion Projections	• Do the team's schedule projections indicate problems? • Has the team planned actions to address these problems?
5	Load Balancing	Is the team rebalancing its workload whenever necessary?

Step	Activities	Review Questions
6	Time Recording	Are the engineers using the time recording log to record their time?
7	Task Recording	Are the engineers recording when they complete each project task?
8	Size Recording	Are the engineers properly recording their size data?
9	Defect Recording	• Are the engineers properly recording their defect data? • Are they using the defect recording log?
10	Reviews	• Is the team conducting all of the required reviews and inspections? • Are the engineers using and updating their personal review checklists?
11	Review Rates	Is the team meeting its review rate plan?
12	Ratios	Is the team meeting its phase and defect ratio plans?
13	Yield	Is the team meeting its phase and process yield plan?
14	Defect Density	Is the team meeting its defect density plan?
15	Test Defects	• Is the team's estimate of final test defects reasonable? • Is the planned test time adequate for finding these defects?
16	Benchmarks	How does the team's performance compare with the benchmark teams?
17	Management Actions	At the conclusion of the review • Summarize the actions to be taken. • Verify that the team leader will write a brief review report. • If management actions are needed, check that responsibility is assigned. • Summarize the improvements you will look for in the next review. • Compliment the team and the team leader for the work they have done.
Exit Criteria		• The appropriate review stage topics have been covered. • Action items have been defined, reviewed, and assigned. • The meeting report responsibility has been assigned.

mistake and that engineers, like anybody else, are often defensive about their errors. Any discussion of who makes the most errors or of defect ratings implies an intent to assign blame. If the engineers on any team think management is looking for the engineers who inject the most defects, even the best engineers will feel threatened. Then no engineer anywhere in the entire organization will accurately report any of his or her defect data.

In gathering defect data, engineers generally will record inspection defects first, then test defects. They are not as willing to record the defects found in personal reviews, and they often object to recording the defects found in compiling. Although all defect data are important, don't insist on getting everything at once. When the engineers start recording inspection and test defect data, also ask about the review and compile defects. Emphasize that effective quality management requires complete defect data and that you expect your teams to gather and use these data.

As long as you and the other managers keep requesting defect data and using the data properly, at least some of the engineers will start to gather that data. With continued emphasis, more engineers will comply and then more of them will see the usefulness of the defect data. When most of the team reaches this point, defect data gathering should become routine.

STANDARD-STAGE REVIEWS

When the team is doing a reasonable job of making and following plans and gathering process data, move to the standard-stage questions. While you should normally start any review with a few of the initial-stage questions described in Appendix D, those topics are not repeated here. The topics to address in a standard-stage review are covered by questions 9 through 16 in the lower sections of the Quarterly Review Checklist in Table E.1.

In the following discussion, we again use the example of Janet's project.

Defect Charts

In answering your questions about defects, Janet shows the data in Figure E.2. She explains that this defect-removal profile shows that the team is not meeting its defect-removal goals and that the reason for this must be one or more of the following:

1. Since the project has not yet been completed, many of the components have not been developed, so their defects could not yet be found.

2. The engineers may not be recording all of the defects that they find.

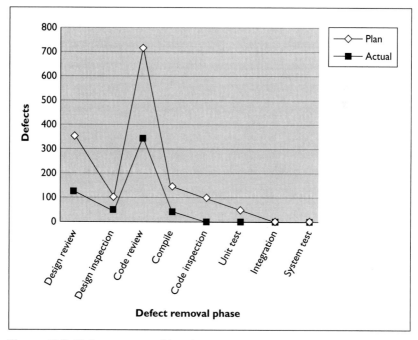

Figure E.2 Defects removed by phase

3. The engineers may not be finding the defects that are there.

4. The engineers may have injected fewer defects than anticipated.

Janet explains that it took her some time to figure out which of these cases applied. Since this study revealed useful information, she next reviews what she did. The first chart Janet shows is Figure E.3, a run chart of compile defects by module. A run chart shows a time sequence of events as they occur. In this case, the event is compiling a module.

In discussing this chart, Janet explains that it shows the compile defects per KLOC recorded by the engineers when they compiled their modules. For example, runs number 1 and 2 had zero reported defects, as did the modules in runs 5, 10, 15, and 17. The upper limit line is the TSP guideline for compile defects,

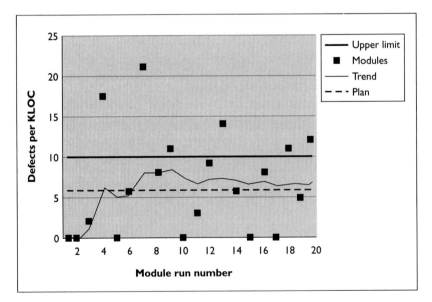

Figure E.3 Compile defect run chart

and the plan line shows the team's quality plan. The trend line gives the team average of compile defects per KLOC to date. Janet explains that, since fewer defects are better, low run chart values would be good if the defect data were accurate. Also, she explains that when compile defects per KLOC are above the upper limit, the module is likely to have quality problems.

To find out whether the zeros on Figure E.3 indicate that no defects were found or that the engineers did not record the defects, Janet next looked at the code review data. By doing code reviews, engineers find most of their defects before they compile or test. When they do not review the code or review too quickly, they find few, if any, defects before compiling and testing. Janet is concerned about compile defects because this is the first objective measure of the quality of the engineers' work. With these data, she will see quality problems early and can correct them before the start of testing. Without this information, she could not identify defective modules until later, and then the team would likely spend months in test, instead of the few weeks they had planned.

Questions on Review Rates

The TSP uses code reviews to find defects early in development. In doing a code review, an engineer first prints a program listing and then reviews the printed code. While this sounds "low tech," it is actually the most efficient way to find defects in programs. A program listing looks much like a column of phone numbers and addresses in a phone book, except that each entry is a program instruction. The TSP uses LOC per hour to measure review rate, and a 200 line-of-code program takes about four pages of text.

To appreciate the importance of finding defects early, see Figures E.4 and E.5, which show Xerox data on the time required

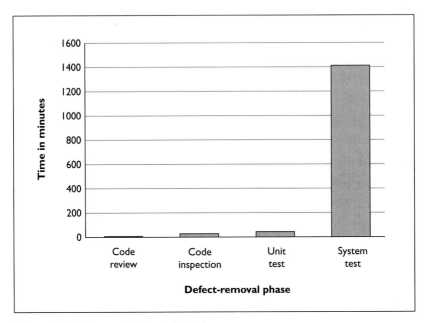

Figure E.4 Time to find and fix defects

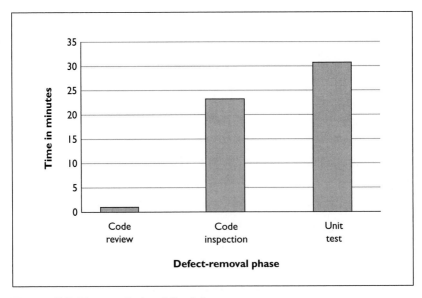

Figure E.5 Time to find and fix defects

to find and fix defects in code reviews, code inspections, unit testing, and system testing [2]. The code reviews averaged about 2.0 minutes per defect, while it took an average of 1,405 minutes (or 23 hours) to find and fix each defect in system test. This is somewhat faster than typical code review rates, which run between 6 and 12 minutes per defect.

To identify the high-risk modules, Janet next looked at code review rates, as shown in Figure E.6. This is a run chart of code review rates for the modules shown in Figure E.3. Since careful reviews take time, low values are good. To compare the two charts, she plotted the modules in the same order on both run charts. She also showed the data in tabular form in Table E.2.

Janet was most concerned about module 1, because it had a high review rate and zero compile defects. She talked to the engineer who developed that module and he admitted that he had

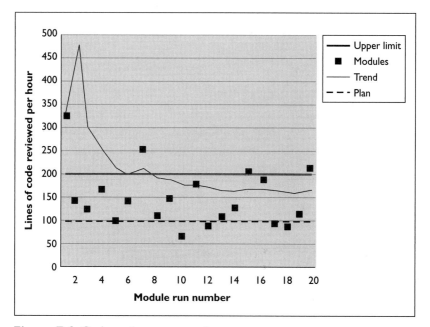

Figure E.6 Code review rate run chart

Table E.2 Module Review and Defect Data

Module Number	Compile Defects/KLOC	Code Review Rate LOC/hour	High Risk Modules
1	0	328	**
2	0	143	
3	2	126	
4	18	168	??
5	0	98	
6	6	143	
7	21	251	**
8	8	109	
9	11	146	??
10	0	68	
11	3	179	
12	9	89	
13	14	106	??
14	6	128	
15	0	208	**
16	8	184	
17	0	93	
18	11	88	
19	5	111	
20	12	218	**
Plan	6.27	100.12	
Upper Limit	10.0	200	

done much too fast a code review and that he had not recorded any of his compile defects. He promised to take more time in his next reviews and to record his defect data.

The other modules with high review rates were 7, 15, and 20. Also, modules 4, 9, and 13 had high compile defect levels. Janet talked to all these engineers, and they agreed to be more careful doing their code reviews. The programmer for module 15 also admitted to not recording compile defects; but she refused to do so, because she didn't think that code reviews were important and felt that recording defects was a waste of time. Janet told her that the project was doing reviews and that she must as well. Since she then agreed to do code reviews, Janet decided not to insist on the defect data just yet. However, Janet would watch her work closely and if her review rates did not meet the team's goals or her modules had many test defects, she planned to talk to her again.

Questions on Phase and Defect Ratios

As shown in Table E.3, the TSP provides guidelines for various defect stages and ratios. While these ratios are not hard rules, in total they provide a useful picture of the quality of the engineering work. For example, in a code review, the guideline suggests that an engineer who spent four hours coding a module should spend at least two hours doing the code review. This may seem like a lot of time, but the Xerox data show that this time is more than recovered by shorter testing times. The other phase ratios show whether or not engineers are spending enough time producing designs and doing design reviews.

Similarly, the defect ratios and levels show whether or not the engineers are removing most of the defects before compiling and testing.

Questions on Yield Management

The yield measure refers to the percentage of the defects removed in a phase or group of phases. For example, the TSP defines the yield-before-compile measure as the percentage of the defects removed from a program before it is first compiled.

Table E.3 TSP Phase and Defect Ratio Guidelines

Guideline	Explanation
Detailed design time >= coding time	Engineers should spend at least as much time in detailed design as in coding.
Design review time >= 50% design time	Engineers should spend at least half as much time reviewing their designs as producing them.
Code review time >= 50% coding time	Engineers should spend at least half as much time reviewing their code as they spent producing it.
Design review defects >= 2*unit test defects	Engineers should find twice as many defects in design reviews as in unit testing.
Code review defects >= 2*compile defects	Engineers should find twice as many defects in code reviews as in compiling.
Compile defects <= 10 per KLOC	High compile defect stages indicate either poor or no code reviews.
Unit test defects <= 5 per KLOC	High unit test defect stages indicate either poor code reviews or design problems.

Similarly, the yield-before-unit-test measure gives the percentage of defects removed before unit test.

With the TSP, early attention to quality removes most defects before testing begins. Therefore, a typical TSP project will have less than 0.5 defects per KLOC in system test and require little time in test. Figure E.7 shows Xerox data on the impact of the TSP on system test duration [2]. Before using the TSP, Xerox typically spent 30% to 50% of the project schedule in system test. When using the TSP, they spent about 10%.

In answer to your questions on yield, Janet explains that her team's quality plan has process yields of 81.9% before compile, 97.3% before unit test, and 99.2% before system test. While

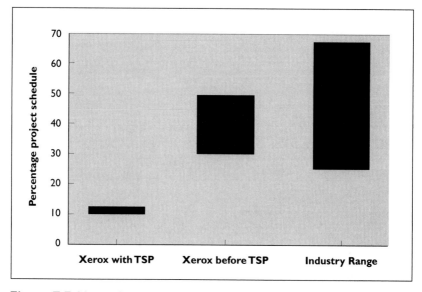

Figure E.7 Xerox data on system test time

these numbers are aggressive, other TSP teams have achieved similar yield values. To achieve this quality, the team set a goal of finding 70% of each module's defects during the code review and inspection phases. Because many engineers achieved higher yields during PSP training, Janet feels they can do this on the project. If they do, she is confident they will meet the quality plan and spend only a few weeks in system test.

Janet has not yet calculated preliminary yield values because she needs the test data to make the calculations. However, she will calculate preliminary yield values once more modules have completed unit test. This will help her understand the quality of the engineers' work and the likely quality of the finished product.

Questions on Defect Density

In discussing defect density, Janet explains that she has data on only a few modules. She also cautions that these data must be kept in perspective. For example, module 8 had 16.3 defects per

KLOC in unit test—more than treble the guideline for unit test shown in Table E.3 and well above the team's plan. This high number surprised her because the compile data for this module looked good. When she talked to the engineer, he explained that module 8 had only 123 LOC and only one defect in compile (he had misspelled a file name). However, he had made a couple of simple design mistakes that were so obvious that he didn't see them during the design or code reviews. For such a small module, 2 defects in unit test looks like very poor quality. Janet concluded that this engineer was striving to produce quality programs and that this module would likely not be a problem.

Defects are essentially random. Very capable engineers make a few mistakes, even when they use disciplined methods. Since these defects must show up someplace, they will be found in the modules. If even a single defect occurs in a small module, the defects per KLOC will be large. For example, if a program module of 123 LOC had 2 defects in unit test, this would be 16.2 defects per KLOC, which is well above the TSP unit test guideline of 5 defects per KLOC. If the compile defect per KLOC value was near 10 or below and the engineer spent enough time in design, design review, design inspection, code review, and code inspection, the module is not likely to be a problem. However, if the engineer did not report compile defect data or spent inadequate time in the design, review, or inspection phases, the component should be carefully checked.

Janet then explains that the reason she is so concerned about unit test defects is that high defect rates imply that the tested product will have many remaining defects. In general, unit testing will only find about 50% of the defects in poor quality products. Therefore, if her team finds 250 defects in unit test, there would probably be about 250 defects left to be found in final testing. Since it generally takes about 2 to 3 engineer days to find and fix each defect in final testing, quality problems would almost certainly cause her to badly miss her schedule commitment.

Questions on Benchmarked Comparisons

Benchmarks can be helpful for motivating improvement. By comparing one team's performance with that of other TSP teams, the engineers can see where improvement is possible. You can also compare the performance of the sub-teams on larger TSP multi-team projects. Because others have achieved the benchmark values, the engineers are more likely to accept them. If your organization has used the TSP before, you will likely have prior team data to use as a benchmark. If not, other organizations are using the TSP, and they may be willing to serve as benchmarks. There is also a growing volume of published TSP results.

Have your teams compare their performance on review rates, phase ratios, yields, and defect densities with the benchmark teams and explain the differences. If your teams are not striving for better work, see if you can motivate them to do so. If they are striving for aggressive goals but not making them, encourage them to continue, and ask if there is anything management can do to help. If the goals appear to be too aggressive for a first step, suggest that they set intermediate goals. The objective is not to strive for unachievable goals but to focus on gradual and continuous improvement.

SUMMARY AND CONCLUSIONS

The following eight principal points are made in this appendix:

1. The objective of the standard-stage review is to maintain a continuing team and management focus on quality.

2. In conducting a standard-stage review, follow the Quarterly Review Checklist.

3. At the standard-stage, the focus is first on the defect data and then on the quality measures.

4. If there are more than a few problems with defect data gathering, focus on improving this area before moving on to the other questions.

5. When teams have satisfied the standard-stage criteria, motivate them to use their data for benchmarked improvement.

6. Benchmarked improvement should continue indefinitely.

7. At the end of the review, ask for a summary of the actions to be taken, and verify that someone is assigned to handle each one.

8. Close the meeting by summarizing the principal topics that you will look for in the next review, and thank the team and team leader for their efforts.

REFERENCES

1. Allen P. Nikora. "Error Discovery Rate by Severity Category and Time to Repair Software Failures for Three JPL Flight Projects." Software Product Assurance Section, Jet Propulsion Laboratory, 4800 Oak Grove Drive, Pasadena, CA 91109-8099, November 5, 1991.

2. Private communication from Allen Willett, a PSP instructor and TSP coach at Xerox.

F
Return on Investment

This appendix provides the backup material for the example return-on-investment (ROI) discussion in Chapter 8. The specific numbers used in this calculation are hypothetical, but they are typical of the costs and benefits organizations have experienced from using the TSP.

SUMMARY OF IMPROVEMENT RESULTS

A Software Engineering Institute (SEI) study describes the TSP results from 4 organizations and 28 projects [1]. These results were mentioned in Chapter 8 and they are shown in Table F.1. Fifteen of these projects used the TSP methods, and 13 did not.

The magnitude of the improvements from TSP introduction is clearer when displayed graphically. The graphs of the quartile ranges* are shown in Chapter 8 in Figures 8.1 through 8.5 on pages 93 through 97.

Return on Investment Savings Assumptions

The ROI calculation assumes that your organization has 100 software engineers, plus associated managers and support personnel.

---

* The quartile range shows the performance of the middle 50% of the population. It omits the top and bottom 25%.

Table F.1 Summary of TSP Results

Category	Without TSP	With TSP
Effort deviation (% average, range)	16% −60% to +100%	−4% −36% to +26%
Schedule deviation (% average, range)	33% −33% to +157%	6% −8% to +23%
System test defect density (defects/KLOC, range)	1 to 8	0.1 to 1.1
Acceptance test and release defect density (defects/KLOC, range)	0.2 to 1.9	0 to 0.35
Duration of system test (days/KLOC, range)	1 to 7.7	0.1 to 1.1

It also assumes that the engineers work on project teams with an average size of 10 engineers. This group has 10 team leaders and several senior managers and executives. Presumably, there are also small departments for quality assurance, testing, computing facilities, advanced technology, and an SEPG (Software Engineering Process Group). Such an organization is shown in Figure F.1.

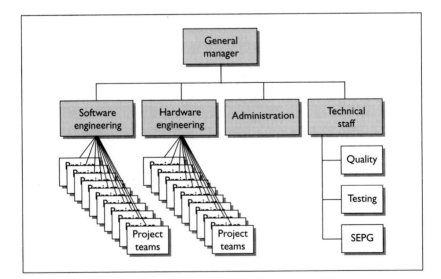

Figure F.1 Example software organization

Table F.2 TSP Savings Assumptions

Item	Current	TSP
Test time as a percentage of total development time	40%	10%
Delivered defects/KLOC	5	0.5
Defect repair time (engineer days)	1.5	1.5
Engineer working days per year	250	250
KLOC developed per year	400	

The savings in the ROI calculations result from the test-time reductions and product quality improvements found by TSP users. These savings are shown in Table F.2. The logic for the assumptions used is described in the subsequent paragraphs.

Test time as a percentage of development: This example assumes that test time is 40% of the normal project schedule. This may seem like a large number, but it is actually lower than many organizations currently experience. For example, as shown in Figure E.7 on page 193, Xerox test time before TSP introduction averaged from 30% to 50% of the development schedule. Also, Microsoft has about one test engineer for every developer, and their development engineers probably spend between 25% to 50% of their time running tests or supporting testing. Therefore, Microsoft's testing costs probably range between 60% to 75% of total development.

To judge the reasonableness of the 40% test time figure, the typical percentage of development time spent in test can be estimated by CMM maturity level.* While I know of no published

---

* The Capability Maturity Model (CMM) is briefly described in the footnote on page 65 in Chapter 6.

data on this subject, the typical test times that I have observed by maturity level are roughly as follows:

- CMM level 1: 40% to 60%
- CMM level 2: 35% to 40%
- CMM level 3: 30% to 35%
- CMM level 4: 25% to 30%
- CMM level 5: 20% to 25%

With the TSP, testing time is typically reduced by 7 to 10 or more times, even when the organization is at a high-maturity level. For example, Hill Air Force Base was the first U.S. government organization to reach CMM level 5. The average time that the Hill projects spent in integration and system testing was 22% of the development schedule. The first TSP project at Hill achieved a value of 2.7%, or an 8 times reduction in the testing schedule [2]. Similarly, at Boeing, which has many high-maturity groups, one TSP project reduced testing time by 94% [3]— a 16 times reduction! In this chapter, I have assumed that the TSP reduces testing time by 75%, or only 4 times. This would cut testing time from the 40% shown in Table F.2 to 10% of the development schedule.

Delivered Defects/KLOC: The defect densities in delivered commercial software typically range from 1 to 10 or more defects per KLOC. Without a focused quality program, delivered defect levels are often about 5 defects per KLOC, which is the value assumed here. With the TSP, delivered defect levels are very low, and zero in many cases. In this example, we assume that delivered defect levels are reduced by 10 times to 0.5 defects per KLOC, or slightly above the highest number found in the SEI study [1].

Defect Repair Time: Here the assumption is the same for the TSP and non-TSP cases. The value selected is the same as Teradyne's experience, or 1.5 engineering days per defect found in final testing, field testing, or by the users.

Working Engineer Days per Year: The assumption here is that all engineers work the same 40-hour week, 50 weeks of the year, whether using the TSP or not. This is 250 working days per year.

KLOC Developed per Year: The example assumes that the ten engineering teams are developing application programs and that they currently deliver about 400 KLOC of software per year. While the KLOC developed per engineer-year will vary considerably depending on the type of work being done, the absolute productivity level does not affect the ROI calculations. No assumption is made for the LOC developed per year under the TSP. That number is determined as part of the savings calculations.

INTRODUCTION STRATEGY

To estimate the costs of introducing the TSP, you should first estimate the training, support, and expert assistance required. To do that, you must decide on the introduction strategy. For example, for faster introduction, you will need more expert assistance. Conversely, if you immediately train some of your own people to be PSP instructors and TSP coaches, they could handle most of the PSP and TSP introduction work. Since they would need less outside help, this would minimize your introduction costs. You will ultimately need these coaches and instructors anyway, so this would be a sound investment.

The Minimum Time Introduction Strategy

To introduce the TSP in minimum time, many organizations strive to train everyone quickly. This is not recommended. The TSP is not a training program; it is a program to change the behavior of organizations. The objective is to transform your operation into a disciplined, planned, measured, and quality-controlled engineering organization that consistently delivers quality products on schedule and for their planned costs.

While you could train all of your people very quickly, changing everyone's behavior takes time. Your organization will not accept and follow the TSP management principles until you do. Once it is clear to your managers that you are serious about the TSP, however, they will adapt to the new methods rather quickly. Those few who cannot adapt will soon leave.

To change the behavior of the engineers, TSP introduction includes 10 to 14 days of PSP training and a 4-day team launch. Then, assuming that the teams are properly led, coached, and managed, the engineers' behavior will change. However, this change requires that managers know how to lead, guide, and monitor their teams. When properly trained and supported by qualified coaches, most managers can become effective TSP team leaders.

While TSP management training can be completed in a few days, the managers will not consistently follow the TSP practices unless their executives require them to. This in turn means that the executives must know how the managers should behave and regularly monitor their performance. This last item is the principal determinant of TSP success. When executives provide proper direction and oversight, the TSP can be introduced quickly.

To fully introduce the TSP into this example organization, four internal TSP instructor/coaches are trained and assigned to the technical staff. These people would help provide PSP training and TSP team coaching. The required training for the total organization is shown in Table F.3. The 11-step strategy for rapidly installing the TSP is shown in Table F.4.

The 4-day team launches and periodic 3-day relaunches are part of the projects; these activities are not training. From the time you start until you are ready to launch the first TSP project, a total of $21\frac{1}{2}$ consecutive days of training are required, not including instructor and coach training. Even though these courses can be overlapped and involve different people, scheduling problems generally stretch this time to four to six months.

The Minimum-Cost Introduction Strategy

For a minimum-cost introduction, you would follow the same 11 steps but in a slightly different order. Start with steps 1 and 2, but then train the resident TSP instructor/coaches in steps 6, 8, 9,

Table F.3 TSP Training Requirements

Course	Attendees	Duration	Prerequisites
Strategy seminar	Executives and senior managers	$1\frac{1}{2}$ days	None
Manager training	Team leaders and managers	3 days	None
PSP training	Software engineers	14 days	Competent programmers
Personal process training	Other team members	3 days	None
PSP instructor training	PSP instructor candidates	5 days	PSP training and examination
TSP coach training	TSP coach candidates	5 days	PSP instructor qualification
TSP coach qualification	TSP launch observation	4 days	TSP coach training

Table F.4 TSP Introduction Strategy

Step	Activity	Who	Duration
1	Strategy seminar	Executives & senior managers	1½ days
2	Select 2 or 3 initial TSP teams	Executives & senior managers	
3	Train managers	Managers & team leaders	3 days
4	Train other staff	SEPG, QA, & others	3 days
5	PSP training	Engineers	10–14 days
6	PSP training	Internal instructor/ coaches	10–14 days
7	Launch TSP teams	Initial teams	4 days
8	PSP instructor training	Internal instructor/ coaches	5 days
9	TSP coach training	Internal instructor/ coaches	5 days
10	Observe and qualify coaches	Internal instructor/ coaches	4 days
11	Continued training and launches	The remaining teams	Continuing

and 10. After these internal instructor/coaches have been observed and qualified, they can handle the rest of the training and lead the TSP launches with little or no outside support. Since these new instructor/coaches do not yet have coaching experience, however, most organizations choose to get expert support for the initial teams. As the internal coaches and instructors gain experience, the external support can be phased out.

RETURN ON INVESTMENT

Once you have the information to calculate TSP introduction costs and benefits, you can determine the expected return on investment. The following paragraphs describe the costs of introducing the TSP for the example 100-engineer organization, the benefits of the investment, and the return on that investment.

TSP Introduction Costs

The costs of introducing the TSP in a 100-engineer organization are shown in Table F.5. Here, engineering time is assumed to cost $500 a day, management time $1,000 a day, and executive time $2,000 a day. The total cost of external consultants and expert advisors is assumed to be $400,000. While most organizations have spent between $100,000 and $300,000, this example assumes an accelerated TSP introduction schedule with correspondingly more support.

In any case, this example organization would need four full-time people who are trained as PSP instructors and TSP coaches. At 250 working days per year, this amounts to 1,000 engineering days a year, or $500,000. After the initial training and external support costs, these continuing coaching costs are all that is needed to sustain the TSP program. The total introduction costs, including one year of support by internal TSP instructor/coaches, is $1,728,000.

Table F.5 TSP Introduction Costs

Item	People	People Days	Costs ($000)
PSP engineer training	100	1400	700
Instructor/coach training	4	96	48
Manager training	20	60	60
Executive seminars	5	10	20
Coaching support	4	1,000	500
External support			400
Total cost ($000)			1,728

TSP Introduction Savings

By combining these assumptions with the previously assumed defect levels and development rates, the TSP savings calculations are shown in Table F.6.

Total Days Worked: At 250 working days per year, 100 engineers would work a total of 25,000 days a year.

Engineering Days in Test: Since 40% of development time is currently spent in test, the test time per year before the TSP is 10,000 working days. With the TSP, the test time is 2,500 working days. This is a saving of 7,500 working days or a $3,750,000 annual saving.

Engineering Development Days: The engineering days spent in development is the difference between the total days worked and the days spent in test, or 15,000 days before the TSP and 22,500 days after TSP introduction. Just from reduced testing time, the engineers can spend 7,500 more days in development each

Table F.6 TSP Cost Savings

Item	Before TSP	With TSP	Change	Savings ($000)
Total days worked	25,000	25,000	0	
Engineering days in test	10,000	2,500	7,500	3,750
Engineering development days	15,000	22,500	+50.0%	
LOC of code developed per day	26.667	26.667	0	
LOC developed per year	400,000	600,000	+50.0%	
Shipped defects	2,000	200	1,800	
Engineering defect repair days	3,000	300	2,700	1,350
Total savings				5,100

year—an increase of 50.0% in development work with no additional people! This is a significant productivity improvement.

LOC Developed per Year: With this TSP productivity improvement, the LOC developed per year is 50% higher, or 600,000 LOC instead of 400,000 LOC. This assumes that the time required for the engineers to produce code and prepare it for testing is unchanged by the TSP. Because this assumption ignores the TSP benefits of improved planning, measured task-time management, and load balancing, it is conservative.

Shipped Defects: Before the TSP, the assumed defect density of delivered code was 5 per KLOC, which would amount to 2,000 delivered defects per year. With the TSP, the assumed delivered defect density was 0.5 per KLOC for 600 KLOC, or 300 defects. However, the savings are calculated based on the defects shipped with the current workload of 400,000 LOC, which would be 200 defects.

Engineering Defect-Repair Days: The engineering repair costs for each defect were assumed to be 1.5 engineering days. That allows 3,000 engineering days for defect repair before the TSP, or $1,500,000 of annual defect repair costs. With the TSP, the defect-repair costs are 200*1.5 = 300 engineering days, or $150,000 of defect-repair costs, for an annual saving of $1,350,000. If the same 100 engineers were also required to repair these defects, this would further reduce the time available for developing products.

Combining these numbers leads to a total annual savings of $5,100,000 after the TSP is fully in use by the entire 100-engineer organization. This is about three times the total TSP introduction costs of $1,728,000. Therefore, the total TSP training

and external support costs for the entire organization are returned in only four months of full TSP use. These benefits then
continue every year thereafter.

DISCOUNTED RETURN ON INVESTMENT

Because of the lead times required for training, team formation,
and product development, TSP introduction costs occur rather
quickly, whereas the savings accrue over several years. The time
sequence of the various activities assumed in this example is
shown in Tables F.7 and F.8. As is clear from these tables, the

Table F.7 Time Line for TSP Introduction (days)

Year	Executives	Managers	Training	Coaches	Total Days
1	10	60	448	96	614
2			476	1,000	1,476
3			476	1,000	1,476
4				1,000	1,000
5				1,000	1,000
Total Days	10	60	1,400	4,096	5,566

Table F.8 Time Line for TSP Introduction Economics ($000)

Year	Training Costs	External Support	Coaching Costs	Annual Costs	Annual Savings
1	352	240	0	592	0
2	238	120	500	858	1,312
3	238	40	500	778	3,046
4	0	0	500	500	4,595
5	0	0	500	500	5,011
Total	828	400	2,000	3,228	13,964

savings are delayed by one year but then substantially exceed the introduction costs every year thereafter. The principal cost after the first year is for the internal coaching staff to train, launch, and support the engineering teams. In many organizations, these costs can be charged to the projects being coached.

Applying a 6% annual interest rate to these costs and benefits, the present-value costs and savings for a 5-year TSP introduction program are shown in Figure F.2. Here, the present-value 5-year costs are $2,805,810 and the present value savings are $11,151,963, for an ROI of 397%. At a 10% annual interest rate, the 5-year costs would be $2,524,350 and the savings $9,277,230 for an ROI of 368%.

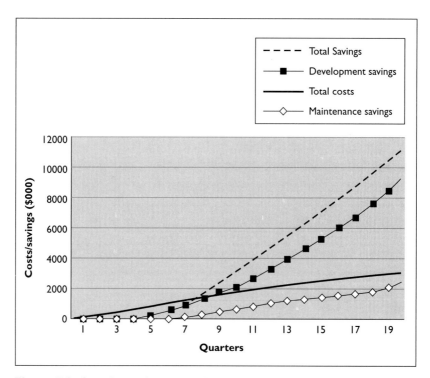

Figure F.2 Cumulative discounted 5-year costs and savings from TSP introduction—6%

SUMMARY AND CONCLUSIONS

The following eight principal points are made in this appendix:

1. Process improvement is an investment, and it should be evaluated in the same way as other investments.

2. The ROI calculations are based on the test-time savings and defect reductions achieved by organizations that have used the TSP.

3. The TSP installation strategy calls for executives and senior managers to first attend a TSP strategy seminar.

4. The next steps are to select the initial teams, train the engineers and managers, and launch the teams.

5. After the initial teams are working effectively, more teams are trained and launched.

6. Internal PSP instructors and TSP coaches should also be trained to handle training of new employees, launch teams, and provide coaching guidance and support.

7. For an example organization with 100 software engineers, the 5-year present-value costs and savings are $2,805,810 and $11,151,963 respectively, which, with a 6% annual interest rate, give an ROI of 397%.

8. At a 10% annual interest rate, comparable costs and savings are $2,524,350 and 9,277,230, with an ROI of 368%.

REFERENCES

1. Donald R. McAndrews. "The Team Software Process (TSP): An Overview and Preliminary Results of Using Disciplined Practices." *Carnegie Mellon University Technical Report* CMU/SEI-2000-TR-015, November 2000.

2. David Webb and Watts Humphrey. "Using the TSP on the Task View Project," *Crosstalk: The Journal of Defense Software Engineering* 12, 2 (February 1999), pp. 3–10.

3. John Vu. "Process Improvement in the Boeing Company." *Proceedings of the 2000 Software Engineering Process Group (SEPG) Conference.* Seattle, WA: Software Engineering Process Group, March 2000.

Index

For Additional Information

Since most groups find it helpful to get experienced guidance in making major organizational changes, the Software Engineering Institute at Carnegie Mellon University provides guidance on the PSP and TSP methods. It also trains engineers and managers to be experts in these methods so that organizations can become self-sufficient. The SEI also licenses collaborating partners who are qualified to assist organizations in introducing these methods. For more information on the assistance available on these methods, see the SEI Web site at http://www.sei.cmu.edu. Additional information is also available at http://www.sei.cmu.edu/collaborating/partners/trans/part/psp/html.

The SEI Series in Software Engineering

CMMI Distilled SECOND EDITION — A Practical Introduction to Integrated Process Improvement — Dennis M. Ahern, Aaron Clouse, Richard Turner — ISBN 0-321-18613-3	**Managing Information Security Risks** The OCTAVE Approach — Christopher Alberts, Audrey Dorofee — ISBN 0-321-11886-3	**The CERT Guide to System and Network Security Practices** — Julia H. Allen — ISBN 0-201-73723-X	**Software Architecture in Practice** Second Edition — Len Bass, Paul Clements, Rick Kazman — ISBN 0-321-15495-9	**The Capability Maturity Model** Guidelines for Improving the Software Process — Carnegie Mellon University Software Engineering Institute — ISBN 0-201-54664-7
CMMI Guidelines for Process Integration and Product Improvement — Mary Beth Chrissis, Mike Konrad, Sandy Shrum — ISBN 0-321-15496-7	**Documenting Software Architectures** Views and Beyond — Paul Clements • Felix Bachmann • Len Bass, David Garlan • James Ivers • Reed Little, Robert Nord • Judith Stafford — ISBN 0-201-70372-6	**Evaluating Software Architectures** Methods and Case Studies — Paul Clements, Rick Kazman, Mark Klein — ISBN 0-201-70482-X	**Software Product Lines** Practices and Patterns — Paul Clements, Linda Northrop — ISBN 0-201-70332-7	**The People Capability Maturity Model** Guidelines for Improving the Workforce — Bill Curtis, William E. Hefley, Sally A. Miller — ISBN 0-201-60445-0
Measuring the Software Process Statistical Process Control for Software Process Improvement — William A. Florac, Anita D. Carleton — ISBN 0-201-60444-2	**Software Design Methods for Concurrent and Real-Time Systems** Hassan Gomaa — ISBN 0-201-52577-1	**MANAGING RISK** METHODS FOR SOFTWARE SYSTEMS DEVELOPMENT — ELAINE M. HALL — ISBN 0-201-25592-8	**MANAGING TECHNICAL PEOPLE** INNOVATION, TEAMWORK, AND THE SOFTWARE PROCESS — WATTS S. HUMPHREY — ISBN 0-201-54597-7	**Introduction to the Personal Software Process** WATTS S. HUMPHREY — ISBN 0-201-54809-7
Managing the Software Process Watts S. Humphrey — ISBN 0-201-18095-2	**The Complete PSP Book** A DISCIPLINE FOR SOFTWARE ENGINEERING — WATTS S. HUMPHREY — ISBN 0-201-54610-8	**Introduction to the Team Software Process** TSPi — Watts S. Humphrey — ISBN 0-201-47719-X	**Winning with Software** An Executive Strategy — How to Transform Your Software Group into a Competitive Asset — Watts S. Humphrey — ISBN 0-201-77639-1	**CMM in Practice** Processes for Executing Software Projects at Infosys — Pankaj Jalote — ISBN 0-201-61626-2
Managing Software Acquisition Open Systems and COTS Products — B. Craig Meyers, Patricia Oberndorf — ISBN 0-201-70454-4	**Architecture-Centric Software Project Management** A Practical Guide — Daniel J. Paulish, Foreword by Len Bass — ISBN 0-201-73409-5	**Cleanroom Software Engineering** TECHNOLOGY AND PROCESS — Stacy J. Prowell, Carmen J. Trammell, Richard C. Linger, Jesse H. Poore — ISBN 0-201-85480-5	**Modernizing Legacy Systems** Software Technologies, Engineering Processes, and Business Practices — Robert C. Seacord, Daniel Plakosh, Grace A. Lewis — ISBN 0-321-11884-7	**Building Systems from Commercial Components** Kurt C. Wallnau, Scott A. Hissam, Robert C. Seacord — ISBN 0-201-70064-6

Please see our Web site at http://www.awprofessional.com for more information on these titles.

Other Books by Watts Humphrey

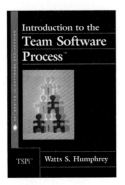

Introduction to the Team Software Process℠
By Watts S. Humphrey

The Team Software Process (TSP) provides software engineers with a framework designed to build and maintain more effective teams. This book, particularly useful for engineers and students trained in the Personal Software Process (PSP), introduces TSP and the concrete steps needed to improve software teamwork.

0-201-47719-X • © 2000 • Hardcover • 496 Pages

Introduction to the Personal Software Process℠
By Watts S. Humphrey

This workbook provides a hands-on introduction to the basic discipline of software engineering, as expressed in the author's well-known Personal Software Process (PSP). By applying the forms and methods of PSP described in the book, you can learn to manage your time effectively and to monitor the quality of your work, with enormous benefits in both regards.

0-201-54809-7 • © 1997 • Paperback • 304 Pages

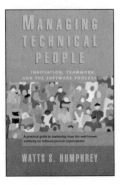

Managing Technical People
Innovation, Teamwork, and the Software Process
By Watts S. Humphrey

Drawing on the author's extensive experience as a senior manager of software development at IBM, this book describes proven techniques for managing technical professionals. The author shows specifically how to identify, motivate, and organize innovative people, while tying leadership practices to improvements in the software process.

0-201-54597-7 • © 1997 • Paperback • 352 Pages

A Discipline for Software Engineering

The Complete PSP Book

By Watts S. Humphrey

This book scales down to a personal level the successful methods developed by the author to help managers and organizations evaluate and improve their software capabilities—methods comprising the Personal Software Process (PSP). The author's aim with PSP is to help individual software practitioners develop the skills and habits needed to plan, track, and analyze large and complex projects, and to develop high-quality products.

0-201-54610-8 • © 1995 • Hardcover • 816 Pages

Managing the Software Process

By Watts S. Humphrey

This landmark book introduces the author's methods, now commonly practiced in industry, for improving software development and maintenance processes. Emphasizing the basic principles and priorities of the software process, the book's sections are organized in a natural way to guide organizations through needed improvement activities.

0-201-18095-2 • © 1989 • Hardcover • 512 Pages